EXPERIMENTING
WITH
ENERGY
CONSERVATION

EXPERIMENTING WITH ENERGY CONSERVATION

BY ROBERT GARDNER

FRANKLIN WATTS
NEW YORK CHICAGO LONDON TORONTO SYDNEY
A VENTURE BOOK

Photographs copyright © : U.S. Department of Energy/Technology Visuals Collection: pp. 11, 41, 43, 48, 109; Comstock Photography: pp. 14 (Russ Kinne), 45 (Georg Gerster); National Renewable Energy Lab: p. 40; Gamma-Liaison/Eric Futran: p. 51; Randy Matusow: pp. 60, 112; FPG International/Robert Bennett: p. 76; The 3M Corporation: p. 89; Photo Researchers Inc.: pp. 98 (Omikron), 123 (Tom McHugh); General Electric Appliances: p. 108.

Library of Congress Cataloging-in-Publication Data

Gardner, Robert, 1929–
    Experimenting with energy conservation / by Robert Gardner.
      p.   cm. — (A Venture book)
    Includes bibliographical references and index.
    Summary: Discusses energy and its conservation and provides experiments with which to investigate the topic.
    ISBN 0-531-12538-6
    1. Energy conservation—Juvenile literature. [1. Energy conservation. 2. Energy conservation—Experiments.
    3. Experiments.] I. Title.
TJ163.35.G33   1992
621.042—dc20   *92-24521*
                                            CIP   AC

CONTENTS

PREFACE

Every month millions of Americans pay billions of dollars for the energy they use. For the heat to warm homes, schools, offices, and factories, for the gasoline to fuel cars, trucks, and buses, for the electricity needed to light streets and buildings and to operate the various electrical appliances that we take for granted. All these require energy. And energy costs money, money that home-owners, businesses, governments, and others who use that energy must pay for.

In this book you'll learn where energy comes from, how it is used, how you can conserve it, and *why* you should conserve it. The investigations you'll carry out will give you an opportunity to experiment with energy, but they will also provide valuable practical experience and knowledge that you'll be able to use for the rest of your life. So let's get started. It's never too soon to start conserving energy!

1

ENERGY CONSERVATION

Experiments show that energy, like matter, cannot be created or destroyed. It can be transformed from one kind to another, but it is never lost or created. Since energy can't be created or destroyed, it is always conserved. We can't help but conserve it! It's a law of nature. So what's all this talk about conserving energy?

When most people speak of conserving energy, what they really mean is, "Use as little energy as possible to get jobs done!" Burn only enough fuel oil to keep your well-insulated house reasonably warm in winter. Drive a car that uses as little gasoline as possible to get you from one place to another. Turn on electric lights and other appliances only when they are needed. Take short showers rather than baths, and, in general, use energy sources as little as possible. This book will use the words *conserve energy* to mean "use as little energy as possible," recognizing that in the true scientific sense we cannot help but conserve energy.

WHY CONSERVE ENERGY? ■ We read in newspapers and magazines that we should conserve energy; radio and television programs urge us to conserve energy. But why should we? Is it a reasonable thing to do?

Most of our energy today comes from fossil fuels—coal, oil, and natural gas. These fuels are the decayed remains of plants and animals that died millions of years ago. We are using these fuels, particularly oil, about a million times faster than they are forming; consequently, we will exhaust our supply of oil within a century or two unless we reduce the rate of use. Coal resources are plentiful, but burning coal pollutes the atmosphere and most scientists recommend reducing our use of coal or finding better, cleaner ways to use it. By conserving energy we give scientists, inventors, and engineers more time to develop other ways of providing energy, ways that will not require fossil fuels.

To meet its huge demand for energy, the United States imports about half the oil it consumes, much of it from the Middle East, where oil is still abundant and easily extracted from the earth. As a result, this country has an unfavorable balance of trade. Monies the U.S. spends on imported goods, particularly oil, exceed

Coal is an example of a fossil fuel (gasoline and natural gas are others). Most of the energy we use comes from fossil fuels.

those it receives from exports by billions of dollars. By using less oil, we could reduce our trade deficit.

When fossil fuels burn, they release carbon dioxide (CO_2) gas into the atmosphere. As a result of the large and growing use of fossil fuels during the last century, the carbon dioxide level in the atmosphere has increased from 290 ppm (parts per million), or 0.029 percent, to 350 ppm, or 0.035 percent. Since carbon dioxide absorbs some of the radiant energy that passes from Earth into space, scientists fear that its continued increase will cause the earth's lower atmosphere to grow warmer. Carbon dioxide "traps" energy much as do the windows in a greenhouse. Consequently, this anticipated increase in atmospheric temperature due to the buildup of carbon dioxide and other gases, such as methane, is often referred to as the *greenhouse effect*. Reducing our use of fossil fuels decreases the rate at which CO_2 is poured into the air. This, in turn, will reduce the greenhouse effect, an effect that could warm the earth, melt the polar ice caps, raise sea level, flood coastal cities, and turn rich farmlands into deserts. Another way to reduce atmospheric CO_2 is to plant trees in large numbers. Trees, like all green plants, absorb CO_2 to carry on photosynthesis; however, to absorb the CO_2 from one 500-MW (megawatt) coal-burning power plant would require 1,000 square miles (2,590 sq km) of forest.

Finally, it makes good financial sense to conserve energy because it will save money. Every family can cut its energy bills by reducing its heating, electrical, gasoline, and other energy use. The more energy you transfer from fuels and power companies to do work in your home and car, the more your family spends. Conserving energy will reduce those costs.

2

MEASURING ENERGY

Energy can't be defined. It's a very complicated, subtle, and elusive concept, but basically, energy enables us to get jobs done. Jobs are done by transforming energy from one form to another or transferring it from one place to another. The chemical energy stored in gasoline can be transferred and transformed into the kinetic energy (motion) of a car when the gasoline burns. The energy stored in a lifted weight can be transformed to kinetic energy when the weight falls. The kinetic energy of such a falling object will be transformed into heat when it strikes the ground and stops moving.

A pile driver uses the energy stored in a lifted
weight to drive large posts into the ground.

Electric energy from a power company can be transferred to an electric motor (kinetic energy) that can lift the weight back to its original position, thereby transforming some of the electric energy into the potential energy stored in the lifted weight. (You've seen that the weight can fall, thereby transforming its potential energy into kinetic energy.) When fuel oil burns, the chemical energy stored in the oil molecules is released. This energy can be transferred as heat from a furnace to an entire house to fulfill the job of keeping the house warm.

We can measure energy in terms of the number of unit jobs done or the amount of fuel used. For example, we could measure the number of kilograms lifted through a given height by an electric motor, or we could measure the number of gallons of gasoline used to move a car from place to place.

In all jobs, forces are exerted and objects are moved from place to place. The energy transferred for any given job is measured in terms of force and distance. The product of the force and the distance through which it acts is called *work*:

$$\text{work} = \text{force} \times \text{distance, or } \mathbf{W} = \mathbf{F} \times \mathbf{d}.$$

If a unit job involves lifting a 1 pound (0.45 kg) weight through a height of 1 foot (0.3 m), then the work transferred to the weight would be

$$\text{work} = 1 \text{ lb} \times 1 \text{ ft} = 1 \text{ ft-lb}.$$

Lifting a 2-pound (0.9 kg) weight through 1 foot requires twice as much work as lifting a 1-pound weight through the same height (2 lb × 1 ft = 2 ft-lb). It is equivalent to lifting a 1-pound weight twice. Similarly, lifting 1 pound through a height of 2 feet (0.6 m) is equal to 2 job units. It is equivalent to lifting 1 pound through a height of 1 foot twice.

For any job, the number of job units required, the amount of work done, and the amount of fuel used are all proportional. To move a car twice as far, or to mow two identical lawns instead of one, requires twice as much gasoline. To lift a weight twice as high requires twice as much work, twice the number of job units, and twice as much fuel.

However, it is possible to use fuel without doing any work. A car at rest with its engine idling transfers no work, but it does produce heat. If you sit idly in a chair or lie in bed, you do no work but your body remains warm. The fuel (food) within your body is "burned" to produce the heat required to keep your body at a temperature of about 98.6°F (37°C). But, as you will see, burning twice as much fuel provides twice as much heat.

UNITS OF WORK, ENERGY, AND POWER ■ As you've learned, work, which measures the transfer of energy, can be measured in units of foot-pounds. It can also be measured in any other unit that is the product of force and distance. For example, a joule (J) of work or energy is the product of a newton (N) of force and a meter (m) of distance:

$$1 \, J = 1 \, N \times 1 \, m.$$

An erg is the product of a dyne and a centimeter:

$$1 \text{ erg} = 1 \text{ dyne} \times 1 \text{ centimeter}.$$

Power is the rate at which work is done. If you walk up a flight of stairs, you do some work on yourself. If you run up the same stairs, you do the same work, but you do it faster—you develop more power. Power is the rate of doing work.

$$\text{power} = \frac{\text{work}}{\text{time}}, \text{ or } \mathbf{P} = \frac{\mathbf{W}}{\mathbf{t}}.$$

Power can be measured in foot-pounds per second, joules per second, ergs per second, or any other unit of work divided by time. A common unit of power used in engineering is the *horsepower* (hp). Another unit widely used to measure the rate of doing work, particularly electric work, is the *watt* (W) or the *kilowatt* (kW).

A watt is 1 joule per second (J/s); a kilowatt is 1,000 J/s:

$$1 \text{ W} = 1 \text{ J/s}; 1 \text{ kW} = 1,000 \text{ J/s}.$$

The man honored by this unit is the Scottish inventor James Watt, the first to use horsepower to measure work. He found that a strong horse could work at a steady rate of about 550 foot-pounds per second. Later, 1 horsepower (hp) was defined as the equivalent of 550 ft-lb per second:

$$1 \text{ hp} = 550 \text{ ft-lb/s}.$$

INVESTIGATION 1: HOW MUCH POWER CAN YOU DEVELOP? □ Is it possible for a human being to develop as much power as a horse? That is, can you or anyone you know transfer energy at a rate of 550 ft-lbs/s, or 746 W (746 J/s)?

To find out, place about 20 to 30 bricks, stones, or other weights on a floor near a covered counter or table. Ask someone to start a stopwatch at the moment you begin lifting the weights one by one from the floor to the table or countertop. The watch should be stopped at the moment you have lifted the last weight. What is the total weight of the objects you lifted? Through what height did you lift them? What is the total amount of work done? How long did it take you to do this work? What was the average power that you developed?

Suppose, for example, that you lifted 20 bricks, each weighing 3.3 lb (15 N), through a height of 4.9 ft (1.5 m) in 30 s. The work you did is

$$(3.3 \text{ lb} \times 20) \times 4.9 \text{ ft} = 320 \text{ ft-lb}.$$

Since you did this work in 30 s, the average power you developed was

$$\frac{320 \text{ ft-lb}}{30 \text{ s}} = 11 \text{ ft-lb/s}, \text{ which is } \frac{11 \text{ ft-lb}}{550 \text{ ft-lb/hp}} = 0.020 \text{ hp.}$$

In metric units, the work done was

$$(15 \text{ N} \times 20) \times 1.5 \text{ m} = 450 \text{ J.}$$

Hence, the power developed was

$$\frac{450 \text{ J}}{30 \text{ s}} = 15 \text{ J/s}, \text{ which is } \frac{15 \text{ J/s}}{746 \text{ W/hp}} = 0.020 \text{ hp}$$

(remember 1 J/s = 1 W).

What power did you develop as you worked? Can you develop more power if you first put the bricks into small piles that you can lift? How much power can you develop now?

Finally, have someone use a stopwatch to measure the time it takes you to run up a flight of stairs. How can you calculate the work you have done? How can you calculate the average power you developed? Did you come closer to working like a horse?

Now repeat the experiment while wearing a knapsack with some weight in it to make you heavier. Can you develop more power when you are heavier?

Some people can develop more than 1 horsepower running up stairs. For how long do you think they could work at such a rate?

ENERGY AND HEAT ■ Early scientists thought of heat as an invisible fluid that flowed from warm objects to cooler ones. Fuels, such as wood and coal, were believed to be chemically combined with the invisible heat fluid, called caloric, so that the fluid was stored in the fuel. When the fuel burned, the caloric was released.

Today, heat is defined as the energy transferred between two objects because of a difference in their temperature. Heat is always transferred from the warmer to the cooler object. The heat that early scientists viewed as something stored in matter is called thermal energy. It is the random kinetic energy (the energy of motion) of the atoms and molecules that make up a sample of matter. The faster the molecules are moving, the more thermal energy they have. The temperature of an object is a measure of the average kinetic energy of its molecules. Thus, a small object may have a high temperature but relatively little thermal energy. A large object, on the other hand, may have a low temperature but lots of thermal energy because it has so many molecules.

19

It is quite easy to transfer energy as heat. If you do work by pushing downward on the piston of a tire pump, the piston will push on the air molecules in the cylinder and make them move faster. Thus, by doing work, you have transferred heat to the gas and its thermal energy has increased. The increase in thermal energy can be detected by a rise in temperature. The average kinetic energy of the gas molecules has increased.

A 10-kilogram mass 1 meter above a floor has potential energy. It is pulled toward the earth by a gravitational force of 98 N. If it falls to the floor, the work done on it will be 98 N × 1.0 m = 98 J. Thus, it can transfer 98 J of energy. If it is allowed to fall slowly by connecting it to a nylon filament wrapped around a stationary copper cylinder, the temperature of the cylinder will rise as the string rubs against it. The potential energy of the mass will be transferred as heat, increasing the thermal energy of the copper. If the mass is doubled to 20 kg, the temperature rise in the cylinder will double when the mass falls. If the mass is halved, the temperature rise in the cylinder will be halved.

If the same mass falls slowly while attached to the hub of a wheel that is free to spin, the wheel will turn and gain kinetic energy as the mass falls. If the mass falls twice as far, the wheel will acquire twice as much kinetic energy. If the mass is doubled and falls twice as far, the wheel will gain four times as much kinetic energy.

A wheel set into motion by the transfer of 98 J of potential energy from a falling mass will acquire almost 98 J of kinetic energy. If the same insulated copper cylinder used before is held against the hub of the wheel, the spinning wheel will transfer heat to the copper as it loses kinetic energy and finally comes to rest. The temperature rise of the copper cylinder will be nearly the same as it was when heat was transferred to it by the falling mass. The thermal energy transferred to the cylinder is the same whether it comes from 98 J of potential energy or 98 J of kinetic energy. Two wheels, each with the same kinetic energy as a single wheel, will transfer twice as much heat. If their combined energy is transferred to the same copper cylinder as before, its temperature will be twice as much.

The potential energy stored in a stretched spring can also be transferred as heat to a copper cylinder. So can the energy stored in a battery. If the poles of a battery or generator are connected to a wire, electric energy will be transferred as heat and the wire will get hot. This is how an electric stove or hot plate works.

Just as all forms of energy can be converted into thermal energy, thermal energy can also be converted to other forms of energy such as kinetic, potential, and electrical. Thermal energy in steam, for example, can be used to give a turbine kinetic energy so that it can produce electrical energy or lift weights. However, it's not possible to transform a given quantity of thermal energy into an equal quantity of another form of energy such as kinetic or potential energy. While 98 J of potential energy can be entirely transferred as heat to the thermal energy of a copper cylinder, the same amount of thermal energy can't be transformed into 98 J of potential energy.

To see why, consider a 1-kg ball of clay at a height of 1 m above a floor. The clay has about 10 J of potential energy. As it falls to the floor, the potential energy is transformed into kinetic energy. When it reaches the floor, the kinetic energy is changed to thermal energy. The temperature of the clay rises. Now, according to the law of conservation of energy, it's possible for all the thermal energy to be changed back into kinetic energy, causing the ball to ascend again to its original height. But from experience, you know that the warm clay will remain on the floor. Its thermal energy is in the random kinetic energy of its billions upon billions of molecules. The likelihood that all these molecules will be moving upward at the same moment is essentially zero. Its molecules are as likely to move down or right or left as they are to move up. Since its molecules are moving in all directions, it doesn't go anywhere.

Fast-moving molecules of steam can push a piston and do work. But some of the steam molecules are also pushing against the sides of the cylinder. No useful work is done here, but the walls of the cylinder do get hot. The molecules of steam transfer some of their thermal energy to the molecules in the cylinder. In any machine where thermal energy is used to do work, some of the thermal energy "rubs off" rather than being transferred to another form of energy.

MEASURING HEAT ■ As far as energy conservation is concerned, we can generally use the early model of heat. That is, we can think of heat as a fluid that flows from warmer to cooler objects. In fact, engineers and scientists frequently talk of heat flowing from one place to another. To find out how heat can be measured, you'll begin by seeing how heat is related to temperature change and mass. The substance you'll use to investigate this relationship is water.

INVESTIGATION 2: MEASURING HEAT □ As a working hypothesis, you can assume that an immersion heater transfers a fixed amount of heat per second. That is, if you plug an immersion heater into an electric outlet, you can assume that it will transfer as much heat during the first 30 seconds it is operating as it will during the second half minute. You can then define one unit of heat to be the heat transferred by the immersion heater in 30 seconds.

Find or buy a 200-W immersion heater like the one shown in Figure 1. Place the heater in 100 g (100 mL) of *cold* tap water in an insulated coffee cup. (You can use volume to measure the mass of the water because the density of water is 1 g/mL.) To give added support to the cup, place it in a glass beaker or tumbler as shown in Figure 1. **Never plug the immersion heater into an electric outlet unless it is immersed in water.** Stir the water before you measure and record its initial temperature. A table like the one below will be useful for recording data in this experiment. Make a similar table in your notebook.

Heat (units)	Mass of water (g)	Initial temperature (°C)	Final temperature (°C)	(ΔT) Change in temperature (°C)	mass x ΔT (g°C)

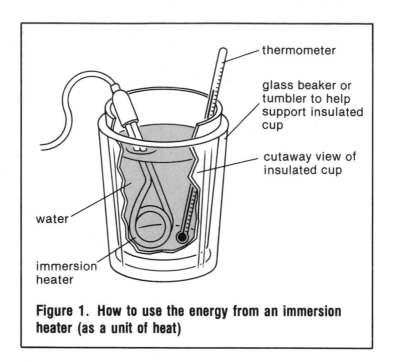

Figure 1. How to use the energy from an immersion heater (as a unit of heat)

Plug the heater into a wall outlet at the same moment that your partner starts a stopwatch or notes the position of a second hand on a clock or watch. Stir the water gently with the immersion heater as the water temperature rises. After exactly 30 seconds, pull the plug from the outlet. **Be sure to grasp the plug, not the cord, when you disconnect the heater.** *Leave the heater in the water* and use it to stir the water until it reaches its maximum temperature. Record this temperature. To find the change in temperature (ΔT), subtract the initial temperature from the final temperature. (The symbol delta, Δ, means "change in.") Why should you leave the heater in the water until you record the final temperature? (If you cannot obtain a thermometer calibrated in degrees Celsius, use a Fahrenheit thermometer.)

To check up on the consistency of the heater, repeat the experiment several times using fresh samples of cold water each time. (You need fresh samples because the warmer the water becomes, the faster it cools off.) If you can read your thermometer to ± 0.5°C, how closely should the temperature changes for the various runs agree if the heater consistently transfers the same amount of heat every 30 seconds?

HEAT TRANSFERRED AND TEMPERATURE CHANGE

How do you think the heat transferred to a fixed mass of water will be related to the temperature change of the water? To test your prediction, deliver 1 unit of heat (the immersion heater plugged in for 30 seconds) to 300 g of cold water in a large (12 or 16 oz) insulated cup. Repeat the experiment, but this time transfer 2 units of heat (plug in the immersion heater for 60 s) to the same amount of cold water. Repeat it once more, transferring 3 units (plug in the immersion heater for 1.5 minutes) of heat to the same mass of cold water, and again to transfer 4 units. Record your data in a table that looks something like this:

Heat (units)	Mass of water (g)	Initial temperature (°C)	Final temperature (°C)	(ΔT) Change in temperature (°C)	mass x ΔT (g°C)
1	300	_____	_____	_____	_____
2	300	_____	_____	_____	_____
3	300	_____	_____	_____	_____
4	300	_____	_____	_____	_____

Use the data to plot a graph of temperature change (ΔT) as a function of the number of units of heat transferred to the water. That is, plot ΔT (the dependent variable) on the vertical axis and heat (the independent variable) on the horizontal axis. The independent variable is the thing you can vary in the experiment. In this case, it is the heat transferred because you can plug the heater in for any period of time you choose. The dependent variable is the quantity that changes in response to changes in the independent variable. In this case, it is the temperature change. What happens to the temperature change as the amount of heat transferred increases?

Look closely at the graph you have plotted. Is the heat transferred proportional to the temperature change of the water? Figure 2 shows a graph plotted from data collected in an experiment similar to yours. As you can see, the slope of the graph is constant and goes through the origin. This indicates that the two variables are directly proportional—doubling the independent variable (the heat transferred) doubles the dependent variable (the temperature change).

HEAT TRANSFERRED AND MASS OF WATER

In the previous experiment, you kept the mass of water constant and found that the change in temperature of the water was proportional to the heat transferred to the water. In this experiment, you'll try to keep the temperature change constant by varying the heat transferred and the mass of water heated. You might predict that to keep the temperature change fixed (or as nearly fixed as experimental errors allow) you would have to

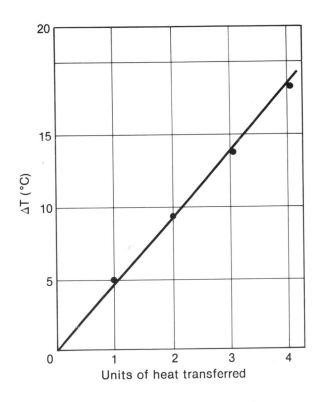

Figure 2. The change in temperature of 300 g of water as a function of the heat transferred to the water by an immersion heater. One unit of heat is the heat transferred by the immersion heater in 30 s

double the mass of the water every time you doubled the heat transferred. If that holds true, then you know that the heat transferred and the mass of water to which it is transferred are directly proportional when the temperature change is fixed.

To test this prediction, you can heat increasing masses of water with increasing numbers of units of heat as suggested in the data table below. Use 8-oz insulated cups for the 100- and 200-g samples of cold water. You'll need 16-oz insulated cups for the 300- and 400-g samples. If you can only obtain 12-oz cups, you'll have to skip the 400-g sample.

Heat (units)	Mass of water (g)	Initial temperature (°C)	Final temperature (°C)	(ΔT) Change in temperature (°C)	mass x ΔT (g°C)
1	100	___	___	___	___
2	200	___	___	___	___
3	300	___	___	___	___
4	400	___	___	___	___

Is the temperature change reasonably constant for each run? If it is, what can you conclude about the relationship between heat transferred and the mass of the water to which the heat is transferred? From the data you have collected, what do you think is the relationship among the variables of heat transferred, temperature change, and mass of water?

To test your idea, determine the product of mass and temperature change (mass × ΔT) for each of the experiments you have made—the last column in the data tables you've recorded. Plot a graph of mass × ΔT as a function of the number of units of heat transferred for each of the runs you've made. Data from a similar set of runs was used to plot the graph shown in Figure 3. What can you conclude?

PREDICTING TEMPERATURE CHANGES

On the basis of the data you have collected and the graphs you have drawn, see if you can predict the temperature changes that will take place in 100 g, 200 g, 300 g, and 400 g of cold water when 1 unit of heat is added to each mass of water. Remember, from your graph you know how much 1 unit of heat is equal to in terms of mass $\times$ ΔT.

Once you've made your predictions, test them by actually doing the experiment and finding the change in temperature of the cold water. How closely do your predictions agree with the actual measurements? Can you suggest another unit for measuring heat, one that need not require an immersion heater?

UNITS FOR MEASURING HEAT ■ As you saw in Investigation 2, the product of the mass and the temperature change of water is directly proportional to the quantity of heat transferred to the water. When 2 units of heat were transferred to the water by leaving the immersion heater plugged in for 1 minute, the product mass $\times$ temperature change was twice as large as it was when only 1 unit of heat was transferred. Thus, we can measure the heat transferred to water by knowing the mass of the water and its change in temperature. We can define a unit of heat to be the heat required to change the temperature of

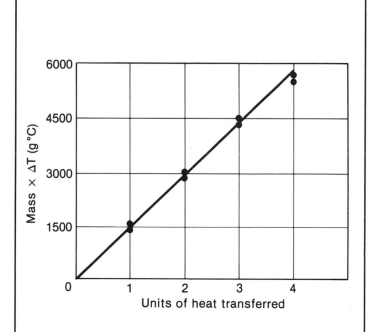

Figure 3. Mass × ΔT as a function of the number of units of heat transferred

1 gram of water by 1 degree Celsius. Such a unit is called a calorie (cal).

$$1 \text{ cal} = 1 \text{ g of water} \times 1°C.$$

If the temperature of 10 g of water changes by 1°C, the heat transferred is 10 cal. If the temperature of 1 g of water changes by 10°C, the heat transferred is also 10 cal. How much heat is transferred when the temperature of 10 g of water changes by 10°C?

Another unit of heat used by heating engineers in the United States is the British thermal unit (Btu). It is defined as the amount of heat needed to change the temperature of 1 pound (lb) of water by 1 degree Fahrenheit.

$$1 \text{ Btu} = 1 \text{ lb of water} \times 1°F.$$

Since there are 454 g in a pound and $1°F = \frac{5}{9}°C$,

$$1 \text{ Btu} = 454 \text{ g} \times \frac{5}{9}°C = 252 \text{ cal.}$$

Table 2-1 on page 32 shows how energy units can be converted to other units.

SPECIFIC HEAT ■ A calorie or a Btu is defined as the amount of heat needed to raise a certain mass of water through a certain temperature change. Suppose you use something other than water, cooking oil for example. If you transfer the same amount of heat to equal masses of water and cooking oil, will the temperature change be the same? Investigation 3 will help you to answer this question.

Table 2-1 Converting energy units

To convert energy in units of	to units of	multiply by
Btu	calorie (cal)	252
calorie	Btu	0.00397
kilowatt-hour (kWh)	Btu	3,413
Btu	kWh	0.00029
kWh	joule (J)	3,600,000 (3.6×10^6)
J	cal	0.24
cal	J	4.2
Btu	J	1,058
J	Btu	0.00095
quad	Btu	1,000,000,000,000,000 (1.0×10^{15})
1 ton of coal	Btu	26,200,000 (2.62×10^7)
1 barrel (bbl) of crude oil	Btu	5,600,000 (5.6×10^6)
1 gallon of gasoline	Btu	125,000 (1.25×10^5)
1 gallon of #2 fuel oil	Btu	139,000 (1.39×10^5)
1 cubic foot of natural gas	Btu	1,031
1 cord of wood	Btu	15,000,000 (1.5×10^7)

INVESTIGATION 3: HEAT NEEDED TO CHANGE THE TEMPERATURE OF 1 GRAM OF COOKING OIL BY 1 DEGREE □ In this investigation you'll try to find out how much heat is needed to change the temperature of 1 g of cooking oil by 1°C. You can use the same immersion heater that you used in Investigation 2 to transfer heat to the cooking oil.

To begin, place 100 g of cold water in an insulated cup supported by a beaker or glass tumbler as before. Place the immersion heater and a thermometer in the water. After measuring and recording the initial temperature of the water, plug in the immersion heater. After exactly 30 seconds, unplug the heater and use it to stir the water. Measure and record the final temperature. What was the change in temperature of the water? How many calories of heat does the heater transfer in 30 s?

Now repeat the experiment with 100 g of cooking oil. It will be helpful to have a partner help you with at least this part of the experiment. Since the density of the oil is only about 0.90 g/mL, you'll need about 111 mL of cooking oil to obtain a mass of 100 g if you are using a graduated cylinder rather than a balance. Measure the initial temperature of the cooking oil in the insulated cup. Then have your partner plug in the heater while you hold it in the cooking oil. **Be careful not to let the heater touch the sides of the cup while heating the oil. Stir the oil constantly with the heater while it is plugged in.** Your partner should disconnect the heater after exactly 30 s. Continue to stir the oil with the heater until the thermometer reaches its maximum temperature. What was the temperature change of the cooking oil?

Since you used the *same* immersion heater for the *same* time to transfer heat to both the water and the cooking oil, you know that you transferred the *same* quantity of heat to both liquids. For example, if the temperature of the 100 g of cold water increased from 20°C to 35°C, then you know that the immersion heater transfers 1,500 cal of heat in 30 s (100 g × 15°C = 1,500 cal).

Now, suppose the temperature of the cooking oil increased from 20°C to 50°C—a temperature change of 30°C. Since the 100 g of cooking oil received the same amount of heat as the water (1,500 cal), it must take only

15 cal to change the temperature of 1 g of cooking oil by 30°C. After all,

$$\frac{1,500 \text{ cal}}{100 \text{ g}} = 15 \text{ cal/g}.$$

To change the temperature of 1 g of cooking oil by 1°C must require

$$\frac{15 \text{ cal/g}}{30°C} = 0.50 \text{ cal/g/°C}.$$

From the hypothetical data given here, we see that the heat needed to warm 1 g of cooking oil through 1°C is only half as much as that needed to warm 1 g of water through 1°C. The heat required to change the temperature of 1 g of a substance by 1°C is defined as the *specific heat* of the substance. Therefore, the specific heat of water is 1.0 cal/g/°C. According to the data above, the specific heat of cooking oil would be 0.50 cal/g/°C. Incidentally, 1 cal/g/°C is the same as $\frac{1 \text{ cal}}{g°C}$ because 1 cal/g/°C is the same as $\frac{1 \text{ cal}}{g} \times \frac{1}{°C}$. It's the same principle as

$$\frac{1}{2} \div 3 = \frac{1}{2} \times \frac{1}{3} = \frac{1}{6}.$$

What do you find the specific heat of cooking oil to be according to your experimental results?

Use the same method to find the specific heat of glycol (antifreeze). Again, be careful not to let the heater touch the side of the insulated cup while the liquid is being heated. Stir the liquid continuously with the heater while it is plugged in. What is the specific heat of glycol according to your results?

Design an experiment that will allow you to measure the specific heat of a solid such as iron or copper.

Table 2-2 contains a list of various materials and their specific heats. As you can see, the numerical value of the specific heat is the same whether it is measured in $\dfrac{cal}{g/°C}$ or in $\dfrac{Btu}{lb/°F}$. Can you explain why?

Table 2-2	The specific heats of some common substances	
Substance	Specific heat $\left(\dfrac{cal}{g/°C}\right)$	Specific heat $\left(\dfrac{btu}{lb/°F}\right)$
Water	1.0	1.0
Steel	0.12	0.12
Copper	0.092	0.092
Aluminum	0.21	0.21
Concrete	0.22	0.22
White pine	0.67	0.67
Ice	0.49	0.49
Glass	0.18	0.18
Gypsum	0.26	0.26
Sand	0.19	0.19
Glass wool	0.16	0.16
Air	0.24	0.24

Heating engineers must consider the heat needed to warm each cubic foot of space in a building. This is easily done since both the specific heat and density of air (0.075 lb/cu ft) are known. It takes 0.24 Btu to warm 1 lb of air through 1°F; each cubic foot of air weighs 0.075 lb; therefore, the heat needed to warm 1 cu ft of air through 1°F is

$$0.24 \ \frac{Btu}{lb/°F} \times 0.075 \ lb/cu \ ft = 0.018 \ \frac{Btu}{cu \ ft/°F}.$$

INVESTIGATION 4: THE HEAT AND FUEL NEEDED TO WARM YOUR HOUSE OR APARTMENT □ With the information given in the previous paragraph and in Tables 2-1 and 2-2, you have all the information you need to figure out the following.

1. How much heat is needed to warm the air in your house or apartment by 1°F? To warm the air from 35°F to 65°F?

2. How much of the fuel you use to heat your living space is needed to provide the quantities of heat that you calculated in question 1? (Assume that all the fuel may be converted to heat that will warm your home.)

Make these calculations and save them; you'll need them again in Chapter 5.

3

SOURCES OF ENERGY

The United States, with only 5 percent of the world's population, uses 30 percent of the world's energy. It's not surprising, therefore, that we depend on other countries for part of our energy. The energy we use comes from a variety of sources, but more than 90 percent of it comes from fossil fuels—coal, oil, and natural gas.

FOSSIL FUELS ■ Millions of years ago a warm and humid climate prevailed, and both plants and animals flourished. As these organisms died, the layer upon layer buildup of their decaying remains produced high pressures and temperatures. The chemical changes that took place under these conditions led to the formation of coal, oil, and natural gas. Because these fuels came from ancient plants and animals, they are called fossil fuels.

Of course, the energy stored in fossil fuels came from the sun. These ancient plants, just like plants today, carried on photosynthesis, the process by which green plants combine carbon dioxide and water in the presence of sunlight to produce food. These plants, and the animals that eat them, use the food for energy. Thus, the energy stored in the remains of their tissues (fossil fuels) came originally from the sun.

Oil is the source of most of the energy used in transportation, which accounts for about one quarter of all the energy we use. Industrial processes require about 30 quads (see Table 2-1, page 32) of energy annually, 40 percent of the nation's total energy use. About 26 quads are required for residential and commercial uses. A third of the approximately 76 quads of energy used each year in the United States is in the form of electricity. Of course, electrical energy is a secondary energy source. It is generated in power plants where fissionable uranium (for nuclear power), falling water (for hydroelectric power), wind, and sunlight are the sources of electric energy. However, three-fourths of all our electricity is generated from steam produced by burning fossil fuels, more than half of which comes from coal.

TIDAL ENERGY ■ There are still other ways of generating electricity. The movement of the moon about the earth gives rise to the daily ebb and flow of ocean tides. This movement of water due to lunar motion holds great potential for hydroelectric power. However, there are few sites where it is practical to tap this vast source of energy; construction is costly, and tidal power plants interfere with the movement of fish and the ecology.of the bays, marshes, and estuaries along the shores behind such plants.

ENERGY FROM THE WIND ■ In areas where the wind blows consistently at speeds in excess of 10 mph (16 kph), it is possible to build windmills that generate electricity. During the 1980s, windmills generating more than 1,500 megawatts (MW) of electric power were built, primarily in California. The cost of this wind-generated energy is about seven cents per kWh. Conventional plants using coal can generate power at a cost of about 30 percent less, but the wind power is pollution free.

Of course, it is the uneven heating of the earth by the sun that gives rise to winds. Consequently, wind power is but another form of solar energy.

FROM TRASH TO ENERGY ■ In some regions, a portion of the 5 pounds (2.3 kg) of solid waste discarded per person per day is burned to produce electricity. With more and more landfills being closed, it makes sense to use solid waste as a substitute for fossil fuels in power plants. However, there are problems. The waste must be collected and transported to the plant, and the noncombustible components must be separated. Some of the metallic materials separated can be recycled, but the other useless solids must be discarded somewhere. Finally, the remaining combustible waste must be processed so that it can be handled and emptied into

This wind farm at Altamont Pass,
California, has some 300 electricity-
producing wind turbines.

This solid-waste incinerator in Lake
Buena Vista, Florida, burns trash to produce
energy for nearby Walt Disney World.

combustion chambers. Unfortunately, some of the plastics that are burned produce toxic gases that accompany carbon dioxide up the smokestack, and burning solid waste, like fossil fuels, releases carbon dioxide into the atmosphere.

OCEAN THERMAL ENERGY CONVERSION ■ The surface of deep tropical ocean waters heated by sunlight offers another means of using solar energy. These waters, where surface temperatures of 80°F are 40° warmer than the colder, denser water several thousand feet below, can be used to generate electricity. A low-boiling fluid such as ammonia will boil in pipes near the ocean's surface. The vapor can be used to turn the blades of turbines in a floating power plant. On the other side of the turbine, the gas, under high pressure, is condensed by transferring its heat to the cold water pumped from the ocean's bottom. Only certain tropical sites would be suitable for such plants; long power lines would have to extend underwater to cities far from the plant; and the long-term environmental effects of such a plant might create serious problems.

GEOTHERMAL ENERGY ■ In certain places on Earth, thermal energy developed deep within the Earth's crust rises to the surface in the form of hot water and steam. At several such sites, power plants have been built to make use of this natural source of energy to drive steam turbines that turn electric generators. There are other such natural sites where geothermal energy is available, but often they are so far from centers of population that it is not feasible to build the power lines needed to carry the energy.

The Earth's hot interior provides the steam
to generate electricity at the Geysers,
a geothermal energy plant located in Sonoma
and Lake counties in California.

ENERGY FROM BIOMASS ■ The solar energy stored in wood, sugarcane, corn, and other plant matter can be used as an alternative to more conventional energy sources. In Brazil, large amounts of sugar are fermented to make alcohol, which is used as a fuel for automobiles. The alcohol can be mixed with gasoline (1 part alcohol to 9 parts gasoline) to produce gasohol, a fuel that has been used in the United States particularly in times when gasoline is in short supply.

Plant matter can also be gasified by combining it with air and steam under very high pressure. The gas can then be purified and burned in a .gas turbine to generate electricity. While such an energy source is possible, large amounts of land and water would be required to grow crops in the abundance needed. Small countries like Japan could ill afford the space required, and parts of the world where water is as precious as oil would be forced to choose between growing fuel or food. If they chose fuel, they might not live to use it.

It seems more reasonable to use biomass as an energy source when it is a waste product, as it often is in the paper and sugarcane industries. There are projects under way to tap the methane and other waste products produced by the decay of organic matter in capped landfills. Such products can be burned to generate heat to warm buildings or to generate electricity.

NUCLEAR ENERGY ■ We have seen how to make use of such ultimate energy sources as the sun, lunar motion about the earth, and geothermal energy from the earth's core. There is one other energy source. It is the energy that was stored in atomic nuclei at the origin of the universe,

Fission of uranium atoms is the
energy source for this nuclear power
plant at Turkey Point, Florida.

an event often referred to as the Big Bang. Since the accident at a nuclear reactor in Chernobyl in the former Soviet Union in 1986, which caused many deaths, people have been very concerned about the use of nuclear energy to generate electric power in the United States. Not only is there a danger of radiation leaking from the plant, but the reactors produce highly radioactive waste products that must be stored and transported.

On the other hand, 16 percent of the world's electricity is generated in nuclear reactors. In France, where uranium ores are abundant and fossil fuels rare, about three fourths of the electric energy is generated in nuclear reactors. To date, these plants have an excellent safety record. The dangers in mining coal and the polluting gases and particles released when it burns, have surely caused more deaths than nuclear reactors, but its harmful effects develop less rapidly and are less dramatic. Furthermore, the combustion of coal, which is virtually pure carbon, produces more CO_2 per gram than any other fossil fuel. Nuclear reactors release no CO_2.

In a nuclear reactor, the nuclei of atoms of uranium or plutonium split apart when struck by neutrons, a process called nuclear fission. The smaller nuclei that are left after a larger one undergoes fission have less energy than the original nucleus. It is the difference in the energy of the nuclei before and after many of them fission that accounts for the large amounts of thermal energy available in a nuclear reactor. In fact, the fission of 1 gram of uranium releases 80,000,000 Btu, more than 2,500,000 times the energy released by burning 1 gram of coal.

It is true that vast amounts of energy are available from the fissioning of uranium nuclei; however, the fusion of hydrogen nuclei to form helium, which is the sun's source of energy, can release nearly 100 times as much energy per gram as the fissioning of uranium. If scientists and engineers can learn how to control this process that goes on explosively in stars and went on explosively in the hydrogen bombs developed after World War II, we will have a new means of generating electric power. Because there are large amounts of hydrogen on earth, it is not surprising that research on this subject is being pursued enthusiastically by many scientists.

SOLAR ENERGY ■ Although we are 150,000,000 kilometers (94,000,000 miles) from the sun, it is sunlight that prevents the earth from freezing solid. It provides us with energy at a rate of 1,380 watts per square meter, which in one year amounts to 1,500,000,000,000,000,000 kWh of energy—15,000 times the world's energy demand. About 30 percent of this solar energy is reflected back into space, 50 percent is absorbed and reradiated by the Earth, and the rest is used by nature to power the Earth's water cycle. Less than 0.1 percent is used by plants for photosynthesis. There's an abundance of solar energy. Unfortunately, the energy is spread out over the Earth's entire surface, much of it is reflected or absorbed by the atmosphere, and it is available only during the daytime.

At the present time, photovoltaic (or solar) cells have an efficiency of about 12 percent, but research in a number of countries indicates that it may be possible to increase the efficiency two- or threefold. To meet the

Photovoltaic (solar) cells are one means of
exploiting our most powerful energy source,
the sun. This photovoltaic concentrator array
has a peak power output of 2,400 watts.

United States demand for electricity would require about 34,000 square kilometers of photovoltaic cells. This is a large area, but it's only about one-third of a percent of the nation's total land area. However, at the present time, electricity generated in this way costs 25¢/kWh, nearly five times the cost of generating electricity in conventional power plants. Nevertheless, progress is being made. Ten years ago it cost a dollar to generate a kilowatt-hour of electric energy with photovoltaic cells; twenty years ago it cost $60/kWh.

In some parts of Europe, commuters pay to leave their electric-powered cars in parking lots. Before they step into a mass-transit vehicle for the journey to work, they connect their cars' batteries to an electric outlet. While the commuters are at work, the batteries are charged by electricity produced by large panels of photovoltaic cells above the parking lot.

Another method for converting sunlight to electricity is to use mirrors that turn with the sun to focus sunlight reflected from a large area onto a small boiler. Heat from the highly concentrated light is used to boil water that will turn a turbine and generate electricity in a conventional manner. A power plant in the Mojave Desert with a generating capacity of 275 MW uses long, curved troughs shaped something like rain gutters with reflective surfaces to focus sunlight onto a thin pipe that carries oil. The enclosed oil is heated by the sunlight as it is pumped along these long troughs. The hot oil then transfers heat to water in a heat exchanger. The water is changed to steam that is used to drive turbines. Although the cost of electric energy from such plants is two to three times the price of that generated conventionally, the plant itself can be built in less than a year. The construction of most power plants requires six to twelve years.

Although the generation of electricity from sunlight is still expensive, the presence of solar collectors on the roofs of many homes indicates that solar energy can be used to heat water economically, and many new houses are being built with large south-facing windows so that sunlight can be used to heat living space as well as water.

When techniques for generating electricity from sunlight become less expensive, the electricity may be used to produce hydrogen from water. As you probably know, water can be broken down into hydrogen and oxygen by electrolysis. (Hydrogen gas collects at the negative electrode and oxygen at the positive electrode.) Experiments have shown that hydrogen can be used as a fuel for cars. At today's prices, hydrogen cannot compete with gasoline, but in the future, as its cost diminishes and gasoline becomes more precious, hydrogen-powered cars may become popular. Although such cars will never compete with conventional cars in drag races, they will not pollute the air or add to the concentration of carbon dioxide because the product of burning hydrogen is water.

INVESTIGATION 5: SOLAR ENERGY: TEMPERATURES IN SUN AND SHADE □ Tape a thermometer to a sheet of cardboard and put it in a shady place. When the level of the liquid in the thermometer stops changing, record the temperature in the shade. Then place the cardboard sheet and thermometer in bright sunlight. What happens to the temperature? What do you conclude?

Sunlight warms water in these rooftop
solar panels. The hot water produced reduces
the need for other sources of energy.

Someone might argue that the thermometer bulb acts like a lens concentrating the sun's rays to make the thermometer bulb warmer than the air around it. To check up on this idea, build a small cover with tape to shade the thermometer bulb from the sun. Then repeat the experiment. What do you find this time? What do you conclude?

INVESTIGATION 6: SOLAR ENERGY: USING SUNLIGHT TO HEAT WATER

□ Find two identical aluminum pie pans. Paint the inside of one pan with flat black paint. When the paint is thoroughly dry, place a thermometer on the bottom of each of the two pans. Pour 100 mL of cold water, or equal amounts that are sufficient to cover the thermometers, in the two pans. Carefully pull a clear plastic bag over each pan and seal them with tie bands. Put both pans on insulating sheets of cardboard. Record the temperature of the water in each pan before you place them both in bright sunlight.

Watch and record the temperature of the water in the two pans for several hours. Do you see why solar collectors are painted black?

Cover one thermometer bulb with aluminum foil or white paper and the other with an equal amount of black construction paper. What do you think you'll find if you place both of them in bright sunlight or under the light bulb of a study lamp?

INVESTIGATION 7: ELECTRICITY FROM SUNLIGHT

□ Connect a photovoltaic cell to a sensitive ammeter. Then place the cell in bright sunlight or under a lamp. What happens to the meter? What happens when you shade the cell with your hand? What happens when you change the angle between the sun and the cell? How should you turn the cell relative to the sunlight to obtain the maximum reading on the meter?

Project 1: Cooking with Sunlight

You can make a solar cooker out of cardboard, tinfoil, and window glass. Plans for such a cooker are available from Solar Box Cookers International, 1724 11th Street, Sacramento, CA 95814

ENERGY CONSERVATION, THE EQUIVALENT OF AN ENERGY SOURCE ■ Most people don't think of conserving energy as an energy source, but in a sense it is. Every time we use less energy, we use less of some energy source, usually a fossil fuel. Since 1973, the energy required to produce each dollar of gross national product has fallen by 28 percent. This has been possible because industries have practiced energy conservation by plugging steam leaks, by insulating, caulking, taping, and weather stripping buildings, and by developing more fuel-efficient cars. Some experts estimate that conservation, the equivalent of an energy source, could reduce U.S. electric energy needs by as much as one third by the turn of the century.

POWER COMPANIES, ENERGY, AND THE ENVIRONMENT ■ Power companies are often the "bad guys" on environmental and energy issues. They dam rivers and flood scenic areas, they generate nuclear waste, and they burn fossil fuels that increase the amount of carbon dioxide and oxides of sulfur and nitrogen. The CO_2 adds to the greenhouse effect, while the other oxide gases produce more acid rain. Yet the public's demand for electric energy has grown by more than 90 percent in the past two decades. The public wants more electricity, but they don't want nuclear plants and they don't want air pollution. What are power companies to do?

Some power companies have been trying to improve their image and reduce an ever increasing demand for electric energy by sponsoring energy conservation measures for homeowners. New England Electric and other companies have given away efficient fluorescent lights, wrapped fiberglass blankets around poorly insulated hot-water tanks, and installed low-flow shower heads and faucets. Several California power companies plan to cut CO_2 emissions by using solar and geothermal sources of energy rather than fossil fuels. In return for these conservation measures, which cut operating costs, state regulators allow the companies to keep a portion of the savings and pass it on to their shareholders.

4

CONSERVING HEAT AND FUEL

During the winter, one of the major energy costs is the fuel or electricity used to heat the space we live in. If you could heat your house or apartment to 70°F (21°C) on the first cold day and then turn off the heat for the rest of the winter, heating costs would be minimal. Unfortunately, when you turn off the heat source, the temperature in your house begins to fall. You have to continue to supply heat as long as the outside temperature is lower than one that you consider comfortable. To understand why, you need to know something about the way heat flows or is conducted from place to place.

The rate that heat flows from a warm place to a cooler one depends on a number of variables. From your own experience, you know that you feel warmer on a cold night if you curl up under the covers. On a hot night, you shed the covers and lie with your arms and legs spread like a soaring eagle. This might suggest to you that the surface area between the warm object and the cooler surroundings has something to do with the rate at which heat flows.

You also know that as the air temperature drops you feel colder. Perhaps the difference in temperature between the warm object and its colder surroundings affects the rate of heat flow. Furthermore, you probably don't mind standing in the cold for a few seconds, but after a few minutes you become uncomfortable. This suggests that the heat lost increases with time.

INVESTIGATION 8: HOW IS THE RATE OF HEAT FLOW RELATED TO SURFACE AREA?—A QUANTITATIVE EXPERIMENT □ In this investigation you'll do an experiment to see how the rate at which heat flows is related to the surface area through which it flows. You'll need a thermometer, hot water, and two containers that will make the surface area of the water exposed to cooler material very different. Two cylinders, one pancake-shaped and the other a tall, "regular" cylinder, will serve nicely. You can use plastic containers with different diameters for the cylinders.

Use a graduated cylinder to measure out 100 milliliters (mL) of hot tap water (120°F or greater). Pour the hot water into the pancake-shaped cylinder. When the water temperature reaches 110°F, measure how long it takes the water to cool to 100°F. (If you have a thermometer calibrated in the Celsius scale, measure the time the temperature takes to fall from about 45°C to 40°C.) Repeat the experiment with the same amount of water in the regular-shaped cylinder.

How do the times required for the water to fall through the same temperature range compare? In which container does the water temperature fall faster? How do the rates of heat loss, in Btu/s or cal/s, compare for the two containers?

To find out how the surface areas of the water in the two containers compare, you'll need to measure the diameter (or average diameter) of each container and the depth of the water in it. Then you can calculate the surface areas of the two samples of hot water (See Figure 4.) Since the pancake had a large diameter, any errors in its volume measurement probably involved measuring the depth or height of the water. You can check up on this by pouring another 100 mL into the pancake-shaped container and remeasuring or choosing a height that gives just about 100 cm³ for the volume.

In the case of the regular cylinder, the measurements of height are probably more accurate, but if they don't give about 100 cm³ when you use them in the formula ($\pi r^2 H$), remeasure after pouring another 100 mL of water into the cup.

How does the ratio of the rate of heat flow from the two samples of hot water compare with the ratio of their surface areas? If they are nearly the same, then

$$\frac{\text{surface area of pancake}}{\text{surface area of reg. cylinder}} = \frac{\text{rate of heat flow from pancake}}{\text{rate of heat flow from reg. cylinder}}.$$

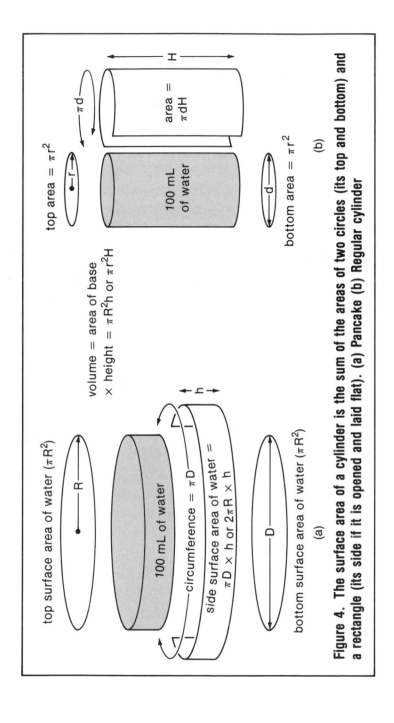

Figure 4. The surface area of a cylinder is the sum of the areas of two circles (its top and bottom) and a rectangle (its side if it is opened and laid flat). (a) Pancake (b) Regular cylinder

and you can conclude that the rate of heat flow is proportional to the surface area through which the heat flows. Of course, there are experimental errors so you can't expect the ratios to be identical. What are some of these experimental errors?

How can you use your measurements of diameter and water depth to confirm the fact that both cylinders contained 100 mL or 100 cm³ of water?

(A milliliter, the unit commonly used to measure liquid volume, and a cubic centimeter, the unit used to measure the volume of solids, are equal.)

INVESTIGATION 9: HOW IS THE RATE OF HEAT FLOW RELATED TO SURFACE AREA?—ANOTHER EXPERIMENT □ You can do another experiment to find the relationship between heat flow and surface area by making two ice "cubes" with different surface areas. Since the heat required to melt a gram of ice is constant, you can determine the rate of heat flow into the ice by measuring the rate at which the ice melts.

To do this, prepare two cylinders of ice. One cylinder should be a wide, flat ice "pancake," the other a regular cylinder of ice. You can use the same two containers you used in the previous experiment. Use a graduated cylinder to measure out and pour exactly 100 mL of water into each container. Place the containers in a freezer. As the water freezes, its volume will increase by about 10 percent so that the final volume of the two pieces of ice will be about 110 cm³.

When the water is thoroughly frozen, which will take several hours, remove the ice from the freezer. After several minutes, you'll be able to remove the ice shapes from their containers and place them on paper

**Think about why ice with holes will
melt faster than ordinary ice.**

towels. Use a ruler to quickly measure the dimensions (diameter and height) of the two cylinders. If the regular cylinder is tapered, measure the top and bottom diameters. The average of the two can be taken to be the diameter of the cylinder.

Dry both pieces of ice with a paper towel. Then, holding one in each hand, place them in a pail of cold water and swirl them under the water for 10 seconds. Remove them from the pail, place them on paper towels, quickly dry them, and place them back in their containers to melt.

While you are waiting for what's left of the ice cylinders to melt, you can calculate what the surface areas of the two pieces of ice were. You can also check to be sure that the dimensions you've measured agree with the known volume of the cylinders (110 cm^3). Remember, the volume of a cylinder is equal to the area of its base times its height. (See Figure 4.) Your measurements should give a volume reasonably close to 110 cm^3 for each cylinder. Since the pancake had a large diameter, any errors in its measurement probably involved measuring its height or thickness. If the water was not perfectly level in the freezer, the thickness may have varied quite a bit. You can check up on this by freezing another 100 mL pancake or choosing a height that gives just about 110 cm^3 for the volume because your measurement of the pancake's thickness was probably not very accurate.

In the case of the regular cylinder, the measurements are probably more accurate, but if they don't give about 110 cm^3 when you use them in the formula ($\pi r^2 H$), remeasure after freezing another 100 mL of water in the cup.

Once the ice has melted, pour the meltwater into a graduated cylinder to see how much of each piece of ice remains. (Remember, 1 g of water = 1 mL.) How many grams of the pancake-shaped piece of ice remain? How many grams melted? How many grams of the regular cylinder melted?

Since the heat to melt a gram of ice is constant and very nearly 80 cal/g, you can determine the amount of heat that flowed into each piece of ice from the mass of ice that melted. For example, if 85 mL of water remain, then 15 g of ice must have melted. Since it takes 80 cal to melt 1 g, the heat that flowed into the ice was

$$15 \text{ g} \times 80 \text{ cal/g} = 1{,}200 \text{ cal.}$$

The rate that heat flowed into the ice was

$$1{,}200 \text{ cal/}10 \text{ s} = 120 \text{ cal/s.}$$

Now you're ready to see if the rate at which heat flows is proportional to the surface area through which it flows. You used a large pail of water to melt the ice so that the temperature difference between the ice and the water would remain very nearly constant. You placed both pieces of ice into the water for the same period of time to keep the time factor constant. You kept the ice in the water for only a short time so that the surface areas of the ice cylinders would not change very much as they melted. Ideally, you'd like to measure the melting rate without any change in area, but from a practical stand-point that's impossible. The surface areas of the cylindrical pieces of ice are given by $2\pi r^2 + \pi dH$ or by $2\pi R^2 + \pi Dh$ as shown in Figure 4.

How does the ratio of the rate of heat flow into the two pieces of ice compare with the ratio of the surface areas of the two pieces of ice? If they are nearly the same, then

$$\frac{\text{surface area of pancake}}{\text{surface area of reg. cylinder}} = \frac{\text{rate of heat flow into pancake}}{\text{rate of heat flow into reg. cylinder}}.$$

and you can conclude that the rate of heat flow is proportional to the surface area through which the heat flows. Of course, there are experimental errors so you can't expect the ratios to be identical. What are some of these experimental errors?

INVESTIGATION 10: HOW IS THE RATE OF HEAT FLOW RELATED TO TEMPERATURE DIFFERENCE? □ Record the air temperature of the area where you'll be working. Then pour hot tap water into a large test tube or a small narrow-mouth jar. Insert a one-hole rubber stopper (or a cork) with a thermometer to seal off the water as shown in Figure 5. If you don't have a cork or stopper, you can use plasticine or modeling clay to seal the opening and support the thermometer. You can support the water-filled test tube with a large lump of clay or a test tube clamp. Record the temperature of the water every minute for an hour or more until the temperature of the water is within a couple of degrees of room temperature.

From the data you have collected, look for temperatures that are about 20°C (40°F) and 10°C (20°F) greater than the temperature of the air into which the heat flows. Choose temperatures that straddle the temperature difference you want by about a degree. For example, in an experiment similar to yours, an experi-

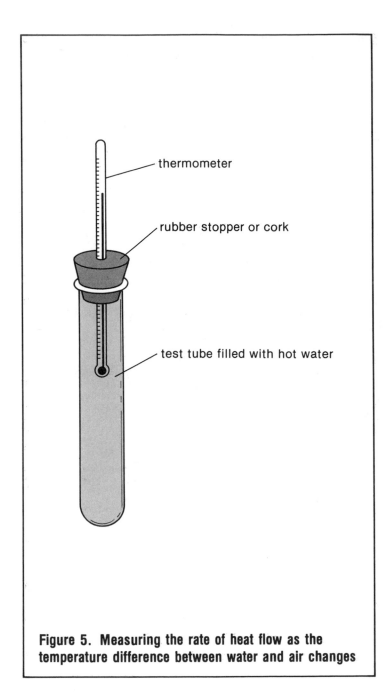

thermometer

rubber stopper or cork

test tube filled with hot water

Figure 5. Measuring the rate of heat flow as the temperature difference between water and air changes

menter working in a room where the temperature was 24°C recorded the following data for temperatures around 44°C and 34°C. Her thermometer had markings at 1° intervals but she estimated temperatures to the nearest tenth (0.1) of a degree.

Time (min)	Temperature (°C)	Time (min)	Temperature (°C)
. . .	. . .	. . .	. . .
2	44.7	22	34.7
3	44.0	. . .	. . .
4	43.2	26	33.1
. . .	. . .	. . .	. . .

Since the mass of the water doesn't change, the heat that it loses to the air is proportional to its temperature change. When the water was about 44°C (20° warmer than the air), its temperature fell from 44.7° to 43.2° in a period of 2 minutes. Its temperature change per minute was about

$$\frac{43.2°-44.7°}{2 \text{ min.}} = -0.75°/\text{min.}$$

What was the temperature change per minute during the period when the water temperature was about 10° higher than the air temperature? How does the rate of heat flow at a temperature difference of 20° between warm water and cool air compare with the rate at a temperature difference of 10°? If the rate of heat transfer is directly proportional to the temperature difference, what should be the ratio of the two rates of heat flow? How do the results from your data compare with that given above? What experimental errors are involved in doing this experiment? What equipment do you need in order to do the experiment with greater accuracy?

For a more detailed look at the relationship between the rate of heat loss and temperature difference, use your data to plot a graph of water temperature as a function of time. Plot the water temperature on the vertical axis and time on the horizontal axis. Then find the slope of the graph at a number of different points as shown in Figure 6. The slope of the graph at each point is a measure of the rate at which heat is transferred from the water. Remember, the mass of the water is fixed so the heat loss is proportional to the temperature change. Of course, you could find the mass of the water in the test tube and calculate the actual heat loss by multiplying the temperature change by the mass of the water.

Once you have found the slope at a number of different temperatures, you can use your data to plot a graph of the rate of heat loss, in °C/min, on the vertical axis and the temperature difference, in °C, on the horizontal axis. To find the temperature difference for each point where you measured the slope, simply subtract room temperature from the water temperature. See Figure 7, where slopes taken from the graph in Figure 6 are plotted against the temperature difference. What can you conclude?

CONDUCTION OF HEAT ■ The flow of heat through a material is called conduction. You have seen that the rate at which heat is conducted through a material is proportional to both the surface area and the temperature difference between the warm matter and the cool matter.

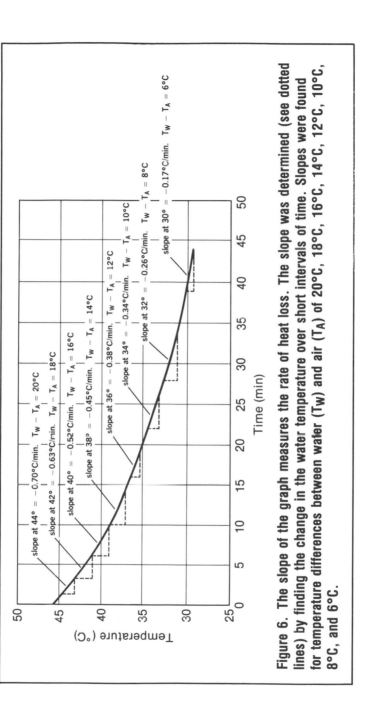

Figure 6. The slope of the graph measures the rate of heat loss. The slope was determined (see dotted lines) by finding the change in the water temperature over short intervals of time. Slopes were found for temperature differences between water (T_W) and air (T_A) of 20°C, 18°C, 16°C, 14°C, 12°C, 10°C, 8°C, and 6°C.

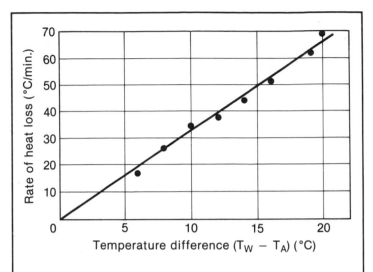

Figure 7. How is the rate of heat loss related to the temperature difference between the warm water (T_W) and the cooler air (T_A)?

Investigations 8, 9, 10, and 11 should have convinced you that this is true.

Is the rate that heat is conducted the same for all materials or does it depend on the nature of the material through which it flows? Investigation 12 will help you answer this question.

INVESTIGATION 11: HEAT FLOW THROUGH DIFFERENT MATERIALS □
Pour 100 mL of hot tap water into a plastic cup. Pour an equal quantity of the hot water into a Styrofoam cup. Cover the plastic cup with a plastic cover through which you have punched a hole to accommodate a thermometer. Cover the Styrofoam cup with a cover made from the lower half of another, similar cup as shown in Figure 8. It too should have a hole through it for a thermometer.

Record the temperature of the water in each cup at 5-minute intervals over a period of 30 minutes or more. (If you have only one thermometer, do the experiment twice, once with each type of cup.)

Through which material does heat flow faster? How do you know? If you plot a graph of temperature versus time using your data for both cups, you'll have a visual comparison of the rate at which the two materials conduct heat.

Place one Styrofoam cup inside another and repeat the experiment. Does the thickness of the material affect the rate at which heat flows through it?

CONDUCTIVITY AND INSULATION ■ Materials such as Styrofoam conduct heat slowly. Such materials are called insulators. Metallic materials, such as copper, are good conductors of heat, which is why cooking pans often have copper bottoms.

To determine the conductivity of a material, heat engineers measure the quantity of heat that is transferred through 1 square foot (0.09 sq m) of its surface per hour per degree of temperature difference between the material and its surroundings. A warm air space surrounded by 10 square feet (0.9 sq m) of ¾-inch (1.9 cm) wood sheathing will transfer 100 Btu of heat in 1 hour when the temperature of the air outside the enclosed space is 10°F cooler than the air inside the sheathing. The conductivity of the sheathing then is 100 Btu/10 sq ft/10°F/h or 1 Btu/sq ft/°F/h also expressed ($\frac{1\ \text{Btu}}{\text{sq ft·°F·h}}$). If the air is enclosed by a ¾-inch layer of mineral wool, the conductivity, or *U value*, is found to be 0.43 Btu/sq ft/°F/h. This indicates that

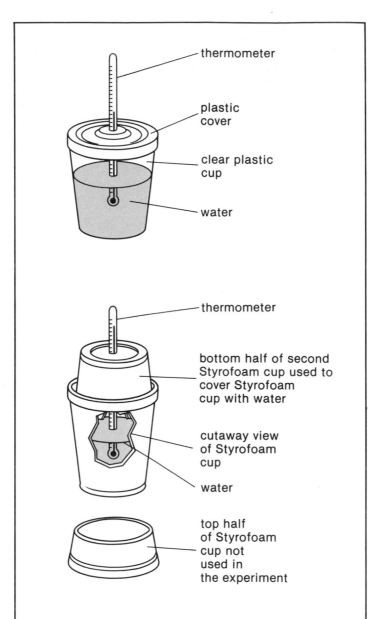

thermometer

plastic cover

clear plastic cup

water

thermometer

bottom half of second Styrofoam cup used to cover Styrofoam cup with water

cutaway view of Styrofoam cup

water

top half of Styrofoam cup not used in the experiment

Figure 8. Does heat flow faster through clear plastic or through Styrofoam?

mineral wool is a better insulator and a poorer conductor than wood sheathing.

The rate of heat flow, or heat transfer, as you've just seen, depends on the conductivity of the particular material through which the heat flows. You've also found that the rate of heat transfer for any material depends on surface area and the temperature difference between the material and its surroundings. Putting this all together we can write

$$\frac{\text{heat transferred}}{\text{time}} = \text{conductivity of the material} \times \text{area} \times \text{temperature difference.}$$

To save space we might write

$$\frac{H}{t} - U \times A \times (T_M - T_S).$$

In this equation H represents the heat transferred, t the time during which it is transferred, U is the conductivity of the particular material, A is the surface area, and $T_M - T_S$ is the temperature difference between the material (M) and its surroundings (S).

If you multiply both sides of the equation by t, the expression becomes

$$H = U \times A \times (T_M - T_S) \times t.$$

From Investigation 2, you know that the heat transferred is proportional to time. An immersion heater delivers twice as much heat in 1 minute as it does in 30 seconds. The results of that investigation confirm the expression written above. In the next chapter you'll use this expression to determine how much heat is required to heat your home for an entire year.

OTHER WAYS IN WHICH HEAT IS TRANSFERRED ■ Heat is transferred from warm bodies to cooler ones in three ways—conduction, convection, and radiation. Conduction involves heat flow by direct contact of molecules. Fast-moving molecules, those with a lot of kinetic energy such as the ones in the warm air of a building, bump into less energetic ones, such as those in the walls. The molecular kinetic energy, which is what thermal energy really is, is transferred to the less energetic molecules. These molecules, in turn, bump into others deeper in the walls and eventually the energy is transferred to the cold air outside.

Heat is certainly conducted from buildings through walls, windows, ceilings, and floors. But heat is also lost by convection, the actual movement of warm masses of material from one region to another. Everyone knows that warm air rises. It is less dense than cold air and so, like a piece of wood released underwater, ascends as cold air moves under it. It is convection that causes air to circulate naturally in a building. Heat is conducted from the air near a cold window, causing the cooled air to sink as its density increases. Air warmed by a radiator near the floor rises as its density decreases.

Heating engineers refer to the cold and warm air that enters and leaves buildings through cracks, chimneys, and open doors and windows as *infiltration*. It's really convection, because the heat is carried by the moving masses of cold air. Poorly constructed houses lose large quantities of heat because of infiltration.

Heat is also transferred by *radiation*. Since there is no air in most of the space between the Earth and the sun, the solar heat we receive cannot travel by conduction or convection. It is transferred from the sun to us by electromagnetic waves like the microwaves that warm food in microwave ovens and the infrared radiation emitted from warm wires, buildings, and your own body.

You can feel heat being transferred to your body if you hold your hand up to the sun or near a fireplace fire. The side facing the sun or flames immediately feels warmer than the surrounding air. If you put your hand below a light bulb and turn on the light, you'll feel heat coming from the bulb immediately. Since the effect is immediate, the heat could not have been transferred to your hand by convection or conduction.

Heat transfer by radiation is proportional to the fourth power of the temperature (T^4). Since the temperatures in most buildings are low in comparison to those in a fireplace fire or the sun, heat losses from buildings as a result of radiation are insignificant compared to those due to conduction and convection.

5

CONSERVING ENERGY BY REDUCING HEAT LOSSES

In Chapter 4 you learned how to calculate the heat transferred by conduction from a warm body, such as a house, to a cooler one, such as the air outside. The heat transferred is proportional to the conductivity of the material through which the heat flows, the surface area, the temperature difference between the warm and cool bodies, and the time the heat flows. All this can be summarized by the equation

$$H = U \times A \times (T_M - T_S) \times t.$$

In this chapter you'll use that information to calculate the annual heat losses from your home or school.

INSULATORS AND R VALUES ■ Builders try to use materials that do not conduct heat well. They want the walls, ceilings, and floors that surround living spaces to have low U values in order to minimize homeowners' heating or cooling costs. To do this, they fill the framed spaces in walls, ceilings, and floors with insulating materials. These insulators are usually rated by their ability to *resist* heat flow rather than their conductivity. The insulating quality of a material, that is, its ability to resist heat flow, is given by its *R value*. The R value of a material is simply the inverse of its U value. For example, in Chapter 4 you learned that the U value of a $3/4$-inch (1.9 cm) layer of mineral wool, is 0.43 Btu/sq ft·°F·h. The R value of the same material is

$$\frac{1}{0.43 \text{ Btu/sq ft·°F·h}} = 2.3 \text{ sq ft·°F·h/Btu.}$$

It's simply the U value turned upside down. The R value indicates that mineral wool is 2.3 times better as an insulator than an equal thickness of wood sheathing, which has an R value of 1.

Materials with large R values are good insulators. Glass-wool blankets 6 inches (15 cm) thick are commonly used to insulate walls. They have an R value of 19. The U value of these blankets is 0.053 Btu/sq ft/°F/h. They're nearly twenty times better insulators than the wood sheathing nailed to the outside of the building's frame because they conduct heat only about $1/20$ as well.

**Insulation placed within a building's frame
significantly reduces heat losses.**

Since $R = \dfrac{1}{U}$, it follows that $U = \dfrac{1}{R}$. The equation for calculating heat losses, which immediately precedes the beginning of this section, may then be written

$$H = \frac{1}{R} \times A \times (T_M - T_S) \times t.$$

This equation is easier to use because the insulating quality of most building materials is given in terms of their R value. Table 5-1 gives the R values of many common insulating and building materials. Notice that air spaces, including the thin air films on interior and exterior surfaces, act as insulators. Why do you think an air film on an exterior surface is a poorer insulator than one on an interior surface?

INVESTIGATION 12: DETERMINING THE R VALUE OF CARDBOARD □ To find the R value of cardboard, you'll need a large cardboard box, a 100-W light bulb, socket, and cord, two thermometers, masking tape, four blocks, and a large nail to punch a hole in the cardboard. Place the light bulb inside the upside-down box in the center of the box's base and **far from any flammable matter** as shown in Figure 9. After you run the cord between the flaps to the outside, seal the flaps shut with masking tape. Place a block under each corner of the box as shown to be sure the entire box is surrounded by air. Use the nail to make a hole in the middle of one side of the box. Slide about half of a thermometer through the hole so that you can measure the temperature inside the box. Use the second thermometer to measure the temperature outside the box.

Table 5-1 R values for common insulating and building materials

Material	Thickness (inches)	R value (sq ft·°F·h/Btu)
Insulating blankets or batts		
Mineral wool	1	3.1
Mineral wool	3.5	11
Mineral wool	12	38
Loose insulation		
Glass fibers	1	2.2
Rock wool	1	2.7
Cellulose fiber (paper)	1	3.7
Vermiculite	1	2.2
Perlite	1	2.7
Expanded polyurethane	1	5.9
Expanded polystyrene	1	4.7
Polyisocyanurate sheathing	1	8.0
Building materials		
Wood sheathing	0.75	1.0
Plywood	0.5	0.63
Gypsum board (Sheetrock)	0.375	0.32
Building paper	—	0.06
Vapor barrier (plastic)	—	0
Wood shingles	—	0.87
Asphalt shingles	—	0.44
Linoleum	—	0.08
Carpet and pad	—	2.1
Hardwood floor	—	0.71
Windows and doors		
Single glazed window	—	1.0
Double glazed window or window and storm window	—	2.0
Double glazed window and storm window	—	3.0
Exterior door	—	2.0
Exterior door and storm door	—	3.0
Masonry		
Concrete block	8	1.1
Concrete block (lightweight)	8	2.0
Concrete, poured	8	0.64
Brick	4	0.80
Air films and spaces		
Air space between building materials	0.75 or more	0.9
Air space between aluminum foil	0.75 or more	2.17
Air film on interior surface	—	0.68
Air film on exterior surface	—	0.17

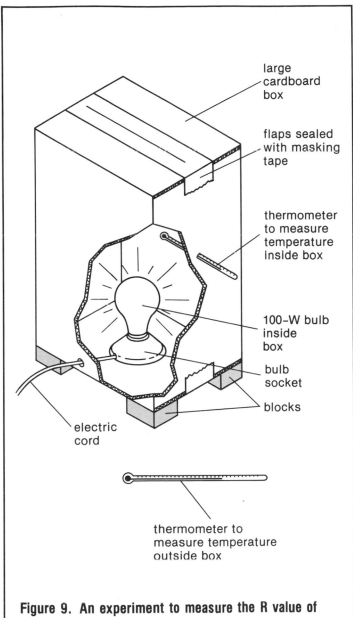

large
cardboard
box

flaps sealed
with masking
tape

thermometer
to measure
temperature
inside box

100-W bulb
inside
box

bulb
socket

blocks

electric
cord

thermometer to
measure temperature
outside box

Figure 9. An experiment to measure the R value of cardboard

Plug in the light bulb and wait until the interior temperature of the box stops increasing. When that happens, you can be sure that heat is being lost from the box as fast as it's being produced inside. Why?

Now you're ready to find the R value of the cardboard. You can use the equation

$$H = \frac{1}{R} \times A \times (T_M - T_S) \times t.$$

Solving the equation for R, you find that

$$R = \frac{A \times (T_M - T_S) \times t}{H}.$$

Since the heat source is a 100-W bulb, we know that it provides 100 J/s. Because there are 3,600 seconds in 1 hour, the bulb will transfer 360,000 J of heat every hour (100 J/s × 3,600 s). From Table 2-1 (in Chapter 2) you see that joules can be converted to Btu's by multiplying by 0.00095. Thus, 360,000 J is equivalent to 340 Btu (360,000 × 0.00095).

Now that the temperature T_M and T_S are constant, like the temperatures inside and outside a house, and the heat that the bulb produces every hour is known, the R value can be calculated once the surface area of the box, in square feet, is determined. Suppose the surface area of the box is 33 sq ft (3 sq m) and the temperatures inside and outside the box are 95°F and 70°F (35°C/24°C) respectively. Then

$$R = \frac{33 \text{ sq ft} \times (95°F - 70°F) \times 1 \text{ h}}{340 \text{ Btu}} = 2.4 \text{ sq ft·°F·h/Btu.}$$

But remember, there is an air film on both sides of the box. Since the box is inside a room, both surfaces are interior surfaces according to the values given in Table 5-1. Thus, the R value for the two air films is almost 1.4 (2 × 0.68). The R value for the air films must be subtracted from the experimental R value of 2.4 to find the insulating factor for the cardboard. Therefore, the R value for the cardboard is 1.0 (2.4 − 1.4). What do you find is the R value of the cardboard box you're using?

How could you use this experiment to measure the *R* values of other materials? **Be sure the light bulb is not close to any flammable matter. If you try good insulating materials, you may have to use a smaller box and/or a less powerful bulb.**

INVESTIGATION 13: THE INSULATING AND BUILDING MATERIALS IN YOUR HOME OR SCHOOL □ In order to find the conductive heat losses for your home or school, you must know what insulation and building materials surround the living space. Many new homes are framed with 2″ × 6″ lumber so that 6-inch batts can be placed between the 2″ × 6″ studs. Older homes and buildings in milder climates often have 2″ × 4″ lumber and 3.5-inch insulating batts. Ceilings may have insulation that is 12 inches or more in thickness. Floors are often less well insulated because basements are generally warmer than the outside air.

Many old homes had no insulation, but owners of such homes may have had cellulose insulation blown into the walls and ceilings. If you can't easily determine the insulating and building materials used in your home or school, ask a carpenter, electrician, plumber, or another craftsman to help you. They can usually find out what materials surround the living spaces in buildings. As a rule of thumb, you can tell if a wall is insulated by placing a thermometer against the inside of a wall whose exterior side is in cold air. If the thermometer reading becomes stable at a temperature 5 or more degrees lower than the center of the room, the wall is probably not insulated.

Once you know what materials are in the building, use Table 5-1 to determine the R value of the *outside* walls (walls adjacent to the outside rather than another room), floors, ceilings, windows, and doors. (Don't forget to include the building materials and air films as well as the insulation.) The inside walls of a building are seldom insulated because most heat is lost through the outside walls. It is the outside walls that are in contact with the cold outside air.

CALCULATING HEAT LOSSES DUE TO CONDUCTION ■ If you know the *R* value of the walls, floors, and ceilings in your house or apartment, their areas, and the temperatures on both sides of these structures, you can calculate the quantity of heat conducted through the building in one hour. For example, suppose the average R value is 15 sq ft-°F-h/Btu, the surface area is 5,000 sq ft, and the average difference between the inside and outside temperature is 30°F. Then the conductive heat losses in 1 hour would be approximately

$$H = \frac{1}{15} \text{ Btu/sq ft·°F·h} \times 5{,}000 \text{ sq ft} \times 30 \text{ °F} \times 1 \text{ h} = 10{,}000 \text{ Btu}.$$

The calculation is easy once the measurements have been made. But, while it's true that the area and R values of the building aren't going to change, the temperature of the air outside certainly will. To measure the temperature and recalculate the amount of heat lost every hour and then add up all the results for an entire year, would be tedious indeed. However, heating engineers found a way to make the task easier; they invented degree-days.

Degree-days are similar to man-hours. One person working for 1 hour constitutes 1 man-hour. One person working for 8 hours is equivalent to 8 man-hours. Ten people working for 10 hours is equal to 100 man-hours.

Since most people agree that a building doesn't have to be heated when the outside temperature is above 65°F, degree-days exist only when the average temperature for the day is below 65°F. Suppose the average temperature on December 31 last year was 40°F. Then for December 31 the number of degree-days was 25. The average temperature for the day is subtracted from 65°F (65 − 40 = 25). If on January 1 the average temperature was 50°F, the number of degree-days for January 1 was 15 (65 − 50 = 15). The total number of degree-days for the two days was 40 (25 + 15).

To find the total number of degree-days for an entire heating season, the degree days for each day in the season are added together. Of course, the number of degree-days in the winter is greater than in the fall or spring, and the number of degree-days in Fairbanks, Alaska, is greater than the number in Miami, Florida. Since degree-day records have been kept for many years, we know the normal number of degree-days per year and per month in various cities across the country.

Table 5-2 shows the number of degree-days that can be expected in Chicago during its heating season. Table 5-3 shows the normal annual number of degree-days for a number of United States cities, and the map in Figure 10 shows how the continental United States is divided in terms of degree-days.

Table 5-2   Heating season degree-days by the month in Chicago, Ill.

Sep.	Oct.	Nov.	Dec.	Jan.	Feb.	Mar.	Apr.	May
81	326	753	1,113	1,209	1,044	890	480	211

Table 5-3   Normal number of degree-days per year for various U.S. cities averaged over thirty years

City	Degree-days	City	Degree-days
Atlanta, Ga.	3,095	Honolulu, Hawaii	0
Boston, Mass.	5,621	Los Angeles, Calif.	2,061
Buffalo, N.Y.	7,062	Miami, Fla.	206
Chicago, Ill.	6,127	Milwaukee, Wis.	7,635
Cleveland, Ohio	6,154	Nashville, Tenn.	3,696
Dallas, Tex.	2,382	New York, N.Y.	4,848
Detroit, Mich.	6,232	Pittsburgh, Pa.	5,987
Duluth, Minn.	10,000	Portland, Oreg.	4,792
Fairbanks, Ala.	14,279	St. Louis, Mo.	4,750
Hartford, Conn.	6,235	Washington, D.C.	4,211
Helena, Mont.	8,129	Wichita, Kans.	4,687

INVESTIGATION 14: THE NUMBER OF DEGREE-DAYS NEAR YOUR HOME □ Use a minimum/maximum thermometer to measure the high and low temperatures each day of the heating season. Assume the average temperature for

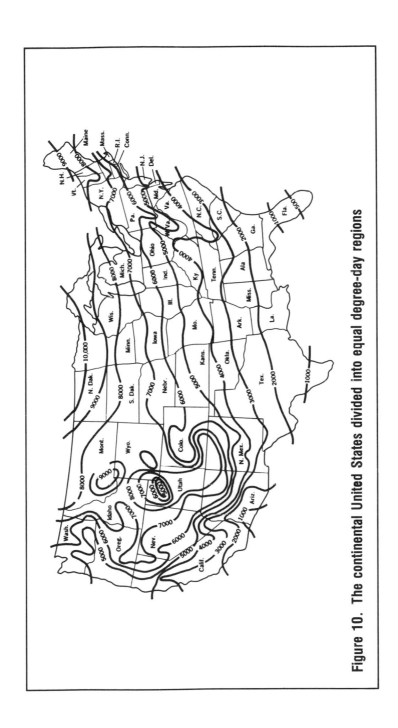

Figure 10. The continental United States divided into equal degree-day regions

each day to be the sum of the minimum and maximum temperatures divided by 2. Keep a careful record of the number of degree-days for each day of the heating season where you live. At the end of the season, add together all the degree-days you have recorded. Compare your results with those given by the weather section of your local newspaper or fuel-supply company. Fuel companies keep up-to-date records of degree-days each year because their customers' fuel needs are related to the number of degree-days.

Based on your records and the normal number of annual degree-days in your region, was the past winter's temperature below average, above average, or normal?

CALCULATING ANNUAL CONDUCTIVE HEAT LOSSES USING DEGREE-DAYS ■ You can use degree-days in place of part of the equation you've used before to calculate heat losses due to conduction. In that equation,

$$H = \frac{1}{R} \times A \times (T_M - T_S) \times t.$$

T_M represents the inside temperature, which is taken to be 65°F for degree-day calculations, and T_S is the outside temperature. Thus, for any single day, the number of degree-days is equal to $T_M - T_S$ where T_S is the *average* outside temperature for the day. The value of t for a day is 24 hours. The conductive heat losses through any surface for a single day can be found by multiplying $\frac{1}{R}$ by the area of the surface, by the number of degree-days ($T_M - T_S$), by 24 hours.

The total number of degree-days for the heating season is the *sum* of all the degree-day values for each day of the season. By multiplying the total number of degree-days by 24 hours, you can convert degree-days to degree-hours and determine the conductive heat losses through the surface for the entire year. For example, using the values from before (5,000 sq ft and R = 15), the annual conductive heat losses in a region where the seasonal heating requirements are 4,000 degree-days (°F-d) would be

$$H = \frac{1}{15} \text{ Btu/sq ft·°F·h} \times 5,000 \text{ sq ft} \times$$
$$4,000 \text{ °F–d} \times 24 \text{ h/d} = 32,000,000 \text{ Btu.}$$

In general, the equation for annual conductive heat losses would be

$$H = \frac{1}{R} \times A \times DD \times 24,$$

where DD is the number of degree-days for the heating season, in °F-d, and 24 is the 24 hours per day used to convert degree-days to degree-hours.

INVESTIGATION 15: CALCULATING THE ANNUAL CONDUCTIVE HEAT LOSSES FROM YOUR HOME OR SCHOOL □ During Investigation 14 you found the R values for the outside walls, the ceilings, and the floors of your home or school. With this information and the number of degree-days in your region, calculate the annual conductive heat losses from your home or school. Don't forget to subtract the area of windows and doors from the wall area. They generally have lower R values than the walls. You'll have to calculate heat losses through the doors and windows separately (see Table 5-1). Then add up all the heat losses to determine the total annual conductive heat losses from your home or school.

HEAT LOSSES FROM INFILTRATION (CONVECTION) ■ Although radiational heat losses from most buildings are not large, infiltration of cold air and the warm air it replaces can exceed conductive heat losses. Few homeowners would be foolish enough to leave their doors and windows open in the wintertime. Nevertheless, spaces around outside doors, cracks in walls, poorly caulked walls and basements, open fireplace dampers, windows that are not properly weather-stripped, and lack of storm doors and windows can account for significant heat losses as warm air is carried away and replaced by cold air.

It is not easy to determine heat losses due to infiltration, but it is generally done by estimating the number of air turnovers per hour. In a new, tight, well-built home with double-glazed windows, insulated doors, and storm doors and windows it probably takes about two hours for the air to turn over once. Therefore, the number of air turnovers per hour, N, is 0.5. A reasonably built home with storm doors and windows, sound caulking, and weather stripping will have about 1 turnover per hour (N = 1). A house with lots of cracks, loose-fitting doors and windows, and no storm doors or windows may have three air turnovers per hour (N = 3).

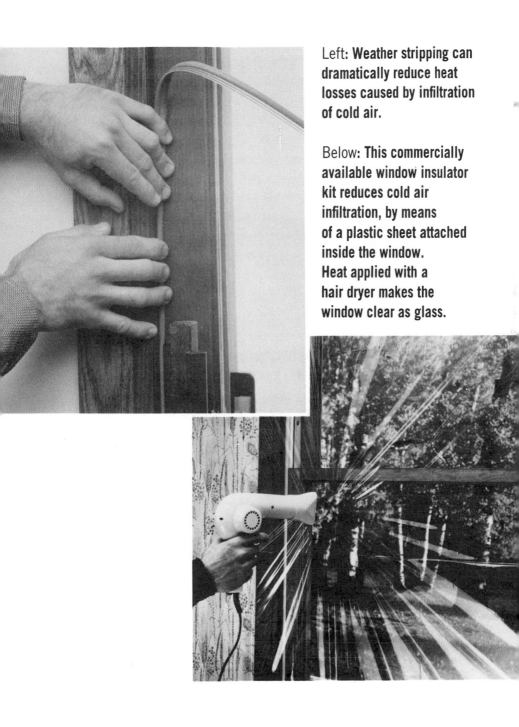

Left: Weather stripping can dramatically reduce heat losses caused by infiltration of cold air.

Below: This commercially available window insulator kit reduces cold air infiltration, by means of a plastic sheet attached inside the window. Heat applied with a hair dryer makes the window clear as glass.

INVESTIGATION 16: CALCULATING INFILTRATION HEAT LOSSES IN YOUR HOME OR SCHOOL □ Every air turnover means that the volume of air in the building must be heated again. Heating the air twice requires twice as much energy as heating it once. Thus a home where the number of air turnovers, N, is 2, will require twice as much heating fuel to meet infiltration losses as a home where N = 1.

Using the guidelines given in the previous section, make an estimate of the number of air turnovers per hour, N, in your home or school. Then measure the inside dimensions of the building—length, width, and height from floor to ceiling (uppermost ceiling if the building has two or more floors)—and calculate the volume of air. In Chapter 2 you learned that it takes .018 Btu to raise the temperature of 1 cubic foot of air through 1°F. How much heat, in Btu's, will be required to raise the air temperature in your home or school through 1°F?

From the estimate you've made of air turnovers per hour, N, and the number of degree-days in your region, you can calculate, roughly, the heat losses due to infiltration using the equation

$$H = V \times 0.018 \times N \times DD \times 24,$$

where V is the volume of the air in the building, in cubic feet, 0.018 is the heat needed to warm 1 cubic foot of air through 1°F, in Btu/cu ft/°F, N is the estimated number of air turnovers per hour, DD is the annual number of degree-days, and 24 is the number of hours per day used to convert degree-days to degree-hours.

For example, suppose the volume of your home is

12,000 cu ft, you estimate N to be 1 turnover per hour, and the number of degree-days in your region is 4,000. Then the estimated annual heat losses due to infiltration would be given by

$$H = 12,000 \text{ cu ft} \times 0.018 \text{ Btu/cu ft/}°F \times 1/h \times$$
$$4,000°F\text{-d} \times 24 \text{ h/d} = 20,700,000 \text{ Btu.}$$

What is your estimate of the annual infiltration heat losses from your home or school?

INVESTIGATION 17: FUEL COSTS □ From Table 2-1, in Chapter 2, you can see that burning a gallon of fuel oil provides about 139,000 Btu of heat; burning a cubic foot of natural gas provides about 1,000 Btu; a cord of wood provides about 15 million Btu; and a kWh of electric energy is equivalent to about 3,400 Btu. If the building you're analyzing has electric heat, the conversion from kWh to Btu is straightforward. However, if it's heated by a furnace that burns natural gas or fuel oil or a by wood stove, the conversion is not 100 percent efficient. It depends on the efficiency of the furnace or stove. If the furnace has been tested recently, you can use the efficiency figure given. If not, assume it's about 75 percent efficient. In that case, a gallon of fuel oil would provide about 100,000 Btu (139,000 × 0.75).

Use fuel or electric bills to find the actual heating costs. If the fuel or electric energy is used for other things, such as heating water, compare bills for winter months with those for summer months to see what percentage of the cost is needed for heating. How much oil, gas, wood, or electric energy was required to heat the building? Given the values for converting the energy stored in fuels or electricity to heat, in Btu, how do your estimates for the sum of conductive and infiltration heat losses compare with the actual quantity of heat used to heat the building?

Since your calculation of conductive heat losses is probably more accurate than the estimate for infiltration losses, you can use your results to revise your estimate for infiltration. In a very tight house, you might find the number of air turnovers to be less than 0.5. On the basis of all the information, what is your revised estimate for N?

INVESTIGATION 18: CONSERVING ENERGY BY REDUCING CONVECTIVE HEAT LOSSES □ It is almost always sound economics to reduce heat losses due to infiltration because weather stripping, electric outlet covers, and caulking are relatively inexpensive. Suppose heat losses due to infiltration are 20 million Btu per year. If you can cut such losses in half, your family or school can reduce heating costs by the equivalent of 10 million Btu, which is about 100 gallons of fuel oil. Multiply the cost of a gallon of fuel oil by 100 and you'll see the savings. The cost of weather stripping and caulking materials will be a small fraction of the money otherwise spent on heating.

On a cold, windy day you can often detect infiltration by simply moving your hand around windows, doors, wall cracks, and electric outlets. You'll feel the cold air moving over your temperature-sensitive fingers. Or you can find air leaks with a draftometer. To make a draftometer, tape one end of a 6-inch-long strip of plastic wrap to a pencil. You'll see the strip move in response to moving air currents.

Once you have located the places where infiltration is present, you can caulk doors, windows, sills, and cracks in the walls, ceilings, and foundation. If you don't know how to apply caulking, ask a carpenter, painter, or handy homeowner to show you. You might also read a how-to book on the subject. Similarly, weather-strip doors and windows where there is infiltration. Usually the packaging that accompanies weather stripping will provide installation instructions. Cold air drafts through electric outlets can be reduced by installing outlet covers or plastic inserts. **If the outlet cover has to be removed, get a knowledgeable adult to help you and to turn off circuit breakers or remove fuses that control the outlet.**

The winter after you have carried out steps to reduce infiltration, compare the ratio of heating fuel used to degree-days for that winter with the previous winter. What do you find? Why do you have to look at the ratio? Why can't you simply compare heating costs or the amount of fuel or electricity used?

INVESTIGATION 19: CONSERVING ENERGY BY REDUCING CONDUCTIVE HEAT LOSSES □ Reducing conductive heat losses by adding insulation to a building is more expensive than reducing infiltration by weather stripping and caulking. Of course, if there is no insulation in the building, then it's almost always cost-effective to add insulation. Begin in the attic. Because warm air rises by convection, the temperature difference is greatest between outside air in the attic and inside air below the ceiling. Placing 12 inches (30 cm) of insulation in such an uninsulated attic will increase the R value from about 2 to 40. How much will that reduce conductive heat losses?

Project 2: Draft Catchers

You may have rooms or spaces in your house, such as a basement, attic, or an unused bedroom that you don't heat in the winter. Look at the bottoms of the doors that open to these rooms. Is there an opening where cold air can come through? If there is, you can reduce that flow of cold air and save heat. You'll need some heavy, colorful cloth, needle and thread, scissors, and some sand. Make a long, thin bag from the cloth. It should be as long as the door is wide. Fill the bag with sand and sew it shut. Lay the sand-filled bag at the base of the door to seal the opening where the cold air comes through. Eliminating the cold air will mean that less fuel is needed to heat it. You've saved both energy and money for your family.

If the attic already has 6 inches (15 cm) of insulation, the payback time (the time it takes to regain the cost of insulating by savings in heating costs) may be too long to merit the expense. How can you decide whether it's worth the money? Similarly, it may be worthwhile to have insulation blown into empty walls, but adding insulation by tearing down the walls and replacing them is seldom economical.

Installing the insulation yourself can save money, but be sure you know how to do it. Talk to the local lumber dealer where you buy the insulation. If not installed properly, moisture may condense in the insulation, causing serious problems. Warm air inside a building in the winter holds much more moisture than the colder air outside. As a result, moisture tends to diffuse from inside to outside, where the concentration is less. If it condenses inside the insulating material, it fills the tiny air spaces, increases the conductivity of the material, and may cause water leaks. To prevent this from happening, a vapor barrier is installed on the *warm* side of the insulation.

Proper ventilation on the cold side of the insulation is also important. It allows the vapor to be carried away. For that reason, attic and soffit vents should *not* be closed. Similarly, the undersides of shingles and clapboards covering outside walls should not be filled with paint. Doing so reduces ventilation and could cause moisture to condense in the walls.

Use the information you have collected to decide whether or not parts of the building you have examined need to be insulated or have more insulation installed. How long will it take to get back in heating-cost savings the money spent on insulation? Discuss your findings with your parents or your school's principal.

INVESTIGATION 20: OTHER WAYS TO REDUCE HEAT LOSSES □ Since heat losses depend on the temperature difference between inside and outside air, it makes sense to turn down the thermostat in a building when people are not there or when they are in beds well insulated by covers. Similarly, unoccupied rooms can be closed off and kept at lower temperatures. Of course, the temperature should be kept high enough so that water does not freeze in pipes. Repairing such damage can be very expensive.

Calculate the reduction in heat losses if thermostats in your home or school are turned down to 50°F (10°C) at night or when people are not present (such as weekends at a school). Calculate also the reduction in heat losses if unused rooms are not heated or kept at cooler temperatures. How much energy will be conserved? How much money can be saved?

6

CONSERVING ELECTRIC ENERGY

Almost every building has electric outlets that enable you to use appliances powered by electricity. The energy is transported to homes and industries by long wires that lead to power plants where giant generators convert kinetic energy to electric energy. At hydroelectric power stations, where about 12 percent of our electric energy is produced, the generators are made to turn by falling water. At other power plants, the energy to turn the generators comes from high-pressure steam. At nuclear power plants, the source of 20 percent of our nation's electric energy, the water

Fontana Dam in North Carolina, a project of
the Tennessee Valley Authority (TVA). This
installation can produce more than 200,000 kw of
electricity. Hydroelectric power plants use
the kinetic energy of falling water to
generate electric energy.

used to make the steam is heated by the energy released when uranium atoms fission. Most of the rest of our electricity is produced by steam from burning fossil fuels.

Electricity accounts for about one-third of all the energy we use. It is a convenient energy source because it can be transmitted great distances by wires that connect homes and industries to the power stations where electric energy is generated. Although hydroelectric plants have an efficiency of about 75 percent, that is, three-fourths of the energy going into the plant is converted to electricity, the efficiency of conventional electric power plants is only about 30 percent. Two-thirds of the energy in these plants is lost as heat that goes up the smokestack or is carried away by the water used to cool the exhaust steam.

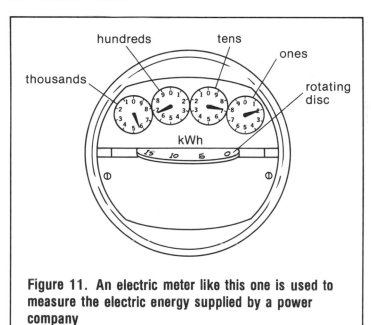

Figure 11. An electric meter like this one is used to measure the electric energy supplied by a power company

METERS FOR MEASURING ELECTRIC ENERGY FROM YOUR POWER COMPANY ■ At each building where a power company provides electric energy, you will find an electric meter like the one shown in Figure 11. If you look at such a meter, you'll see that there is a disk that turns. Electric current, which consists of moving electric charges, makes the disk turn. The disk is connected through gears to a series of dials that are used to measure the electric energy entering the building. The dial on the right records kilowatt-hours of energy, the next dial indicates tens of kilowatt-hours, and so on.

The disk is similar to a car's speedometer. The greater the rate that electric energy is entering the building, the faster the disk turns. The dials are similar to a car's odometer. By subtracting an odometer reading of 25324 at the beginning of a trip from a reading of 25634 at the end, you can find that you have traveled 310 miles. By subtracting a reading of 5172 taken a month ago from the meter reading seen in Figure 11, the power company can tell that you used 500 kWh of energy since the meter was last read. If they charge 10¢ for each kWh, they will send you a bill for $50 for the last month.

MEASURING ELECTRIC ENERGY AND POWER ■ From reading the previous section and Chapter 2, you know that power companies measure electric energy in units of kWh, but what is a kilowatt-hour? Electric energy is carried by electrically charged particles, usually electrons. You can think of these tiny negative charges as coming in bundles. Each bundle carries a certain amount of energy that was generated at the power station. The number of these bundles of charge, called coulombs (C), flowing past any given point per second is called the electric current. Electric current can be measured with a meter. The meter, called an ammeter, is inserted in the wire carrying the current as shown in Figure 12. A flow of 1 coulomb per second (1 C/s) constitutes a current of 1 ampere (1 A).

The energy carried by each coulomb of charge can be measured with another meter, called a voltmeter. The voltmeter—which is connected in parallel with the device that changes the electric energy into some other form of energy such as heat, light, sound, kinetic energy, or any other form—measures the energy per charge in units called volts. A reading of 1 volt (1 V) means that each coulomb carries 1 joule (1 J) of energy that can be transformed into another form of energy in the electrical device. In a light bulb, for example, electric energy is changed into light and heat.

In most household circuits each coulomb of charge carries 120 J of energy. Therefore, these circuits are said to be 120-volt circuits. Suppose the electric current through a certain light bulb is 0.50 A. Since each coulomb carries 120 J, the power rating of the bulb, which is equal to the current times the voltage, is 60 watts (60 W):

$$\text{Power} = \text{current} \times \text{voltage} = 0.50 \text{ A} \times 120 \text{ V} = 60 \text{ W}.$$

You can see that this makes sense because 0.50 A is equivalent to 0.50 C/s and 120 volts is equivalent to 120 J/C. The product of these two readings is 60 J/s or 60 W:

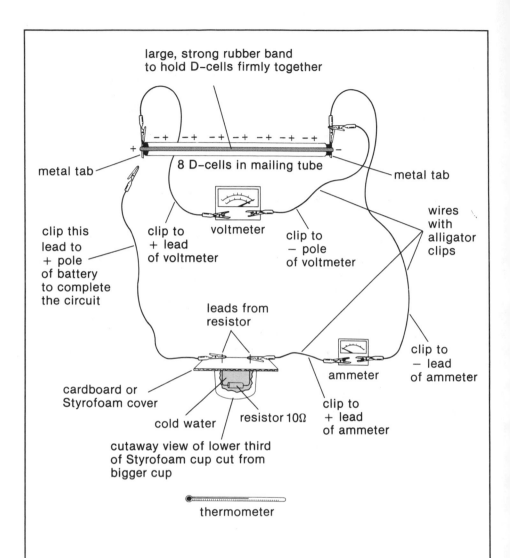

large, strong rubber band
to hold D-cells firmly together

metal tab

— + — + — + — + — + — +

+

8 D-cells in mailing tube

metal tab

wires with alligator clips

voltmeter

clip this lead to + pole of battery to complete the circuit

clip to + lead of voltmeter

clip to — pole of voltmeter

leads from resistor

clip to — lead of ammeter

ammeter

cardboard or Styrofoam cover

cold water

resistor 10Ω

clip to + lead of ammeter

cutaway view of lower third of Styrofoam cup cut from bigger cup

thermometer

Figure 12. This simple electric circuit contains a small heater (resistor) that can be used to warm water. The ammeter in series with the heater will measure the electric current in amperes (A). The voltmeter, which is wired in parallel with the resistor, will measure the voltage—that is, the energy per charge—in volts (V) or joules per coulomb (J/C).

$$0.50 \text{ C/s} \times 120 \text{ J/C} = 60 \text{ J/s}.$$

From the standpoint of units, C divided by C is 1 so that

$$\frac{C}{s} \times \frac{J}{C} = \frac{J}{s} \text{ or W.}$$

This is similar to

$$\frac{3}{4} \times \frac{2}{3} = \frac{2}{4} = \frac{1}{2} = 0.5,$$

or to finding distance from speed and time. For example,

$$40 \frac{\text{mi}}{\text{h}} \times 2 \text{ h} = 80 \text{ mi.}$$

Since power is equal to energy or work per time,

$$\text{power} = \frac{\text{energy}}{\text{time}}, \text{ or energy} = \text{power} \times \text{time.}$$

A 1,000-W bulb transforms 1,000 joules of electric energy to 1,000 joules of light and heat every second. In 1 minute it provides 60,000 J of light and heat (60 s × 1,000 J/s). In 1 hour it provides 3,600,000 J. Since 1,000 W = 1 kW and there are 3,600 s (60 min × 60 s/min) in an hour,

$$1,000 \text{ W} \times 3,600 \text{ s} = 1 \text{ kW} \times 1 \text{ h} = 1 \text{ kWh.}$$

As you can see, 1 kWh is equivalent to 3,600,000 J (1,000 J/s × 3,600 s). To avoid using huge numbers, power companies measure energy in kilowatt-hours rather than joules. A bill for 500 kWh of energy requires fewer numbers and less space and is easier for customers to read than one for 1,800,000,000 J.

INVESTIGATION 21: PREDICTING THE HEAT TRANSFERRED FROM AMMETER AND VOLTMETER READINGS □ Connecting ammeters and voltmeters to 120-volt circuits can be dangerous and should not be attempted. Household circuits contain alternating currents (ac), that is, currents in which the electric charges move back and forth rather than in one direction. With direct current (dc), provided by batteries or dc power supplies that convert ac to dc, the charges flow in only one direction. You can use batteries or a low-voltage power source to provide an electric current and safely investigate a simple electric circuit.

In this experiment you'll transform electric energy into thermal energy and transfer the heat into some cold water. You'll do this by connecting a small heater, called an electrical resistor, to a battery or low-voltage power supply. The final connections should be made only after you're ready to start the experiment. To measure temperatures accurately, you should have a thermometer that can be read to at least ± 0.1°C. This means the thermometer should be marked at least every 0.5°C. If your school does not have such a thermometer, you should recognize that your temperature readings may not be very accurate.

Connect a 10-, 15-, or 20-ohm resistor to a 12-volt battery made from D-cells or to a low-voltage dc power supply as shown in Figure 11. The battery can be made by placing eight D-cells, each of which provides 1.5V, in series (one after the other) as shown. **The resistor**

should not be connected to the battery unless it is submerged in water. Otherwise, it may overheat and be destroyed.

Electric resistors are devices that regulate current; they *resist* the flow of electric charge. Resistors are rated in units called ohms. The resistance of such devices is the ratio of the voltage across their ends to the current they allow to pass: $R = \dfrac{V}{I}$, where R is resistance of the resis-

tor, V is the voltage across the resistor, and I is the current through the resistor.

A ratio of 1 volt per ampere is said to be 1 ohm (Ω). Thus, a 10-Ω resistor will transmit a current of 1 A when the voltage across the resistor is 10 V. It will transmit a current of 2 A when the voltmeter reads 20 V, and so on.

Connect a 0-1- or 0-5-A ammeter in series with the resistor and a 0-15-V voltmeter in parallel with it as shown in Figure 12. Be sure the + and − leads from the meters are properly connected. If a meter needle goes below zero when the circuit is finally connected, immediately disconnect the circuit and reverse the meter leads. The unconnected lead from the resistor shown in Figure 12 should not be connected to the battery or power supply until you are ready to start the experiment.

Pour some cold water into the insulated cup and connect the circuit long enough to measure the current and voltage. How can you use the current and the voltage to determine the electric power?

Assuming that all the electric energy will be transformed into thermal energy, predict the temperature change that you can expect to find for the water if the circuit operates for 2 minutes (120 s). Once you have made your prediction, pour 50 g of cold water (a degree or two below room temperature) into the insulated cup. Stir the water with the thermometer and read the initial temperature to the nearest 0.1° or better. Immediately place the cover on the cup so that the resistor is completely submerged and connect the circuit. After 1 minute, read the ammeter and voltmeter as carefully as possible. The readings should be very nearly the same as the ones you took before. After 2 minutes, disconnect the circuit, stir the water thoroughly with the thermometer, and find the new temperature. Is the temperature change close to the one you predicted from the current, the voltage, and the time (120 s)?

INVESTIGATION 22: PREDICTING THE HEAT TRANSFERRED USING AN IMMERSION HEATER □ Somewhere on the immersion heater you used in Chapter 2 you will find a power rating, probably 200-W. Use this rating to predict the temperature change you can expect to find when 100 g (100 mL) of cold water are heated by plugging the immersion heater into an electric outlet for 30 s. Remember, 200 W = 200 J/s or about 48 cal/s. Since you should use a 120-V circuit, what will be the electric current in the heater?

After you have made your prediction, pour 100 mL of cold water into an insulated cup. Put the immersion heater into the water and carefully read and record the initial temperature. Plug the heater into an electric outlet for exactly 30 s. Stir the water with the heater throughout this 30-s period; then pull the plug. Leave the heater in the water and use it to stir the water so that all the electric energy transformed in the heater can be transferred to the water. What is the final temperature of the water? How closely does the temperature change you have found agree with the temperature change you predicted?

INVESTIGATION 23: THE ENERGY REQUIRED FOR ELECTRIC APPLIANCES □ Your home and school contain a variety of electric appliances—light bulbs, refrigerators, dishwashers, toasters, microwave ovens, radios, TVs, etc. If you look carefully, you'll find a power rating, in watts or kilowatts, written somewhere on each appliance. Make a table listing each appliance and its power rating. Then make an estimate of the number of hours each appliance is used during a one-year period. Use that information to calculate the energy required to operate the appliance for a year. Knowing how much your power company charges per kilowatt-hour, you can also estimate how much it costs to operate the appliance for one year. Table 6-1 shows a partial record for one home where the power company charged 9¢ per kilowatt-hour. (Electric water heaters are one of the most costly appliances, but it's easier to figure their annual operating cost by knowing how much hot water is used. You'll do this in Chapter 7.)

Which appliances are the most expensive to operate? Are they necessarily the ones with the greatest power ratings?

Look carefully at the table you have prepared. Which of the appliances could be used less? For example, could the usage time of the clothes dryer be reduced by hanging clothes on a line? By how many hours could their use be reduced? Which appliances might be replaced with ones that have lower power ratings? Incan-

Table 6-1 A partial listing of electric applicances, their power ratings, usage, energy required, and annual cost

Appliance	Power (watts)	Power (kW)	Time used/ year (h)	Energy/year (kWh)	Cost/year ($)
Coffee maker	1,200	1.20	200	240	21.60
Toaster	1,200	1.20	30	36	3.24
5 light bulbs, 100 w ea.	500	.50	1,100	550	49.50
10 light bulbs, 75 w ea.	750	.75	900	675	60.75
8 light bulbs, 60 w ea.	480	.48	1,400	672	60.48
. . .		. . .	. . .	. . .	. . .	. . .

Energy ratings can help you purchase electrical appliances that will save money in the long run.

More than 90 percent of the electrical energy used by an incandescent bulb produces heat, not light. These light bulbs have been coated with a film that is transparent to visible light but reflects infrared energy back to the lamp in order to greatly reduce the amount of electricity required to heat the filament.

descent bulbs, for example, might be replaced with low-wattage, long-lasting fluorescent bulbs that may be available from your power company. How much money would be saved each year by making these changes?

INVESTIGATION 24: ELECTRIC POWER FROM SUNLIGHT □

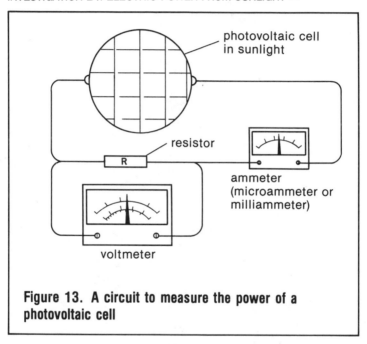

photovoltaic cell
in sunlight

resistor

R

ammeter
(microammeter or
milliammeter)

voltmeter

Figure 13. A circuit to measure the power of a photovoltaic cell

Return to Investigation 7 in Chapter 3 and build a circuit consisting of a photovoltaic cell and a resistor as shown in Figure 13. Place a sensitive ammeter in series with the resistor, and a voltmeter in parallel. You may have to use several resistors and/or meters to find the ones that will give measurements you can read.

What is the power, in watts, developed in this circuit? How many such cells would you need to produce a kilowatt? How would you arrange several such cells to produce a larger voltage?

7

OTHER WAYS TO CONSERVE ENERGY

You've investigated ways to conserve heat and electricity in your home and school—two major energy costs for any building. But if your family owns a car, gasoline is another energy expense. In this chapter you'll explore ways to conserve gasoline and investigate other ways to conserve energy.

CONSERVING ENERGY ON THE HIGHWAY ■
Nearly half of all the oil pumped from the earth is used to fuel the world's 500 million motor vehicles. Every gallon (about 4 l) of gasoline burned in a car's engine produces about 20 pounds (9 kg) of carbon dioxide along with other pol-

luting gases, such as carbon monoxide, hydrocarbons, and nitrogen oxides. During the past fifteen years, more-efficient cars have increased the average miles traveled per gallon and catalytic converters have helped to convert the polluting gases mentioned above to carbon dioxide, water vapor, and nitrogen. However, much remains to be done.

INVESTIGATION 25: MILES PER GALLON □ How far will your family's car go on a gallon of gasoline or diesel fuel? To find out, record the odometer reading the next time the

With fuel prices subject to such large fluctuations, it really pays to buy an energy-efficient car and become familiar with energy-saving techniques.

tank is filled with gasoline. When the tank is nearly empty, see how many gallons it takes to fill it again. What is the odometer reading now? How far has the car traveled since the tank was last filled? How can you calculate how many miles the car traveled per gallon of gasoline?

Make these measurements over several thousand miles to obtain a more accurate estimate of the car's efficiency in miles per gallon (mpg). Make some mpg calculations when the car is used for short trips and in stop-and-go traffic; make some when the car is used for long trips. Under what conditions is your car most efficient? Least efficient?

INVESTIGATION 26: TIRE PRESSURE AND AUTO EFFICIENCY □ You may have heard that underinflated tires can reduce a car's efficiency. To see why, try this experiment with your bicycle. Find a hill that you can coast down to a long, smooth, level or slightly uphill path or road. Try this when the bike tires are inflated to their proper pressure. Mark the point where your bike finally stops along the level path or road. Then let air out of the tires until their pressure is half what it was before and repeat the experiment. How far does the bike coast this time? Can you explain the difference? What evidence do you have to support the idea that cars operating on underinflated tires are less efficient?

INVESTIGATION 27: WEIGHT AND THE ENERGY NEEDED FOR MOTION □ You may have heard that it takes more energy to move a heavy car than a lighter one. To check up on this, ask a small child to sit in a wagon that is at rest on a smooth, level floor, driveway, path, or sidewalk. Use a spring balance to measure the force required to pull the wagon along at a slow steady speed for a distance of 10 feet (3 m) or more. How much work did you do in moving the wagon through the chosen distance?

Now repeat the experiment with a heavy child or an adult in the wagon. How much work did you do this time? In which case did you do more work? What evidence do you have to support the idea that lighter cars require less fuel per mile of travel? In countries where gasoline is very expensive, such as Italy, would you expect to see more light cars on the streets and highways than heavy ones?

INVESTIGATION 28: CARS AND EFFICIENCY □ In this investigation you'll find the drag (retarding force) on a moving car or cars driven by a licensed driver along a smooth, straight, level, lightly traveled section of road or parking lot. Be sure the car's tires are inflated to the recommended pressure. If there is any question about safety in doing the experiment, check with your local police department. They may be able to help you find an appropriate place to do the experiment.

With the car traveling along the smooth, level section of the road at about 40 mph (17.6 m/s), have the driver place the car in neutral. Once the car is coasting, have someone start a stopwatch. This person should say "Go!" when the timing begins and "Now!" at 5-second intervals thereafter for about a minute or until the car is at rest. A second person, sitting beside the driver or looking over his or her shoulder, should state the car's velocity when the timing begins and at each 5-second interval. A third person can record the data. The experiment should be repeated, if possible, with the car going in the opposite direction in case there is a wind or the road is not perfectly level. Start timing when the car is at the same initial velocity as before.

Use the average values from the two sets of readings to plot a graph of velocity on the vertical axis versus time on the horizontal axis. If you'd like to use metric units, 1 mph (1.47 ft/s) is approximately 0.44 m/s. From the slope of the graph, you can find the acceleration of the car (the change in velocity per second) as shown in Figure 14. It will, of course, be negative because the car is slowing down. What does this tell you about the direction of the force?

You'll need to know the mass of the car to find the retarding force (drag). An automobile dealer, car magazines, or consumer guides for cars will have this information. Once you know the car's mass you can multiply it by the accleration to find the force. For example, if the car's mass is 1,500 kg and its acceleration is − 0.20 m/s², then the drag is

$$1,500 \text{ kg} \times (- 0.20 \text{ m/s}^2) = - 300 \text{ N}.$$

Repeat the experiment with the same car after letting some air out of all the tires. What happens to the drag on the car when the tires are underinflated? Be sure to refill the tires with air to proper pressure immediately after the experiment.

How will the car's weight affect the retarding force? One way to find out is to see how far the car will coast before coming to rest with four people in it. Try it in both directions as before. Then repeat the experiment

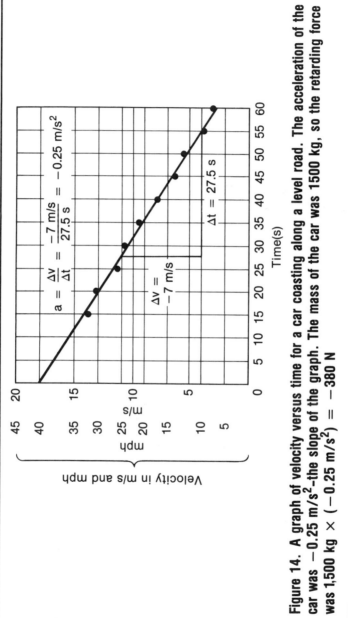

Figure 14. A graph of velocity versus time for a car coasting along a level road. The acceleration of the car was −0.25 m/s²—the slope of the graph. The mass of the car was 1500 kg, so the retarding force was 1,500 kg × (−0.25 m/s²) = −380 N

with only the driver. In both runs, the car should start coasting at the same place and at the same initial speed.

If possible, do the experiment with different cars. Which car seems to have the least drag? The most drag? Does the car's shape (streamline features) seem to affect the drag?

Project 3: Finding Ways to Conserve Gasoline

Conserving gasoline can help reduce our national demand for oil and our negative balance of trade. Form a group to discuss ways in which you can reduce gasoline consumption in your community or region by such means as car pooling, improved public transportation, and better driving techniques. All of these can reduce gasoline consumption, and there are many more. How many can your group think of? How many can you implement?

Project 4: Other Ways to Conserve Energy

The same group might investigate a variety of other ways to conserve energy. For example, there are many ways to improve the efficiency of furnaces and home heating systems; in some moderate climates the installation of heat pumps might reduce energy costs; since windows generally have low R values, your group might design and produce insulated shades or drapes; proper landscaping can sometimes reduce heat losses due to infiltration. What other ways to conserve energy can your group put into action?

INVESTIGATION 29: CONSERVING ENERGY IN YOUR HOME □ You may have seen someone washing dishes or rinsing them before placing them in a dishwasher. Were they using a steady stream of hot water? How much less energy would be needed to rinse the dishes in cold water or to rinse them in a single pan of hot water?

To find out, try rinsing or washing dinner dishes in a stream of hot water. Before you start, close the drain so that you can collect the hot water in the sink. How much hot water did you use? How much did it cost to heat that water?

If, for example, you used 5 gallons (19 l) of water, that's approximately 40 pounds (18 kg). Suppose the water comes into the hot-water tank at 55°F (13°C). It had to be heated from 55°F to the temperature set by the thermostat in the tank. Assume that to be 120°F (49°C). The energy required to heat the water was

40 lb × (120°F − 55°F) = 2,600 Btu or 0.76 kWh (see Table 2-1, in Chapter 2).

How much would it cost to heat this water? How much did it cost in your experiment? Not very much probably, *but* how much would it cost if this were done after every meal 365 days a year?

Using the same approach, estimate how much money can be saved by taking 2- to 5-minute showers rather than baths; by reducing the time spent in the shower; by installing low-flow shower heads.

If you have an electric stove, check the power rating of its oven on the stove or in the owner's manual. How much energy could be saved each year if several foods were cooked in the oven at the same time? When is it possible to do this? When is it not possible? Can energy be conserved by cooking foods in a microwave oven rather than in a stove?

How much money can be saved each year by washing clothes in cold or warm water rather than in hot water? By using a clothesline instead of a dryer? By wearing permanent press clothing, which does not need to be ironed? By insulating hot-water pipes and the hot-water tank? By turning off lights and other appliances when they are not being used? By replacing incandescent bulbs with long-lasting fluorescent ones? (You can check the efficiency by looking at the lumens per watt.) By cooking in covered rather than open pots?

Project 5: Finding Other Ways to Conserve Energy

Form a group to discuss ways in which energy can be conserved in your home or school. One approach might be to think of ways in which energy can be conserved in each room of a home or school. Another approach would be to consider ways of modifying behavior so as to reduce energy use. For example, recycling materials, rather than throwing them away, bypasses energy-intensive steps involved in manufacturing such as converting ores to metal. What approach or approaches will your group take? What will you do to put your ideas into effect?

INVESTIGATION 30: A MODEL SOLAR BUILDING □ If you live in a home or go to a school that has rooms with south-facing windows, notice how warm it is in these rooms on a sunny day. Many homes and offices today are being built to take advantage of the free energy that comes from the sun. In addition to being well insulated, they have large south-facing windows that can be insulated at night and few, if any, windows on the north side.

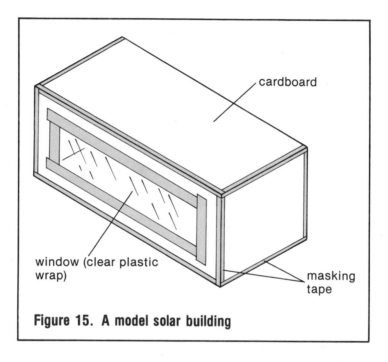

Figure 15. A model solar building

Make a model solar building from cardboard as shown in Figure 15. Place a thermometer on the floor of your building. Seal all joints with masking tape and cover the "window" with clear plastic wrap. The plastic, sealed shut with tape, will allow you to read the thermometer through the window. Take the model outside and leave it in the shade until the temperature becomes steady. Then place it in the sun on an insulating cardboard sheet so that its window faces the sun. Leave the model for 10 minutes; then read the thermometer. What is the temperature now? How much did it increase?

Repeat the experiment, but this time, tape a cardboard cover over the window. After 10 minutes read the thermometer. How much did the temperature increase this time? What do you conclude?

Design your own experiments to find out:

- What effect the direction that the window faces has on the heat transferred to the model building by the sun.
- The effect of the color of the floor on the amount of solar energy transferred to the house.
- The effect of the color of the exterior on the amount of solar energy transferred to the house.
- The effect of insulating the nonwindow portions of the building on the amount of solar energy transferred to the house.

INVESTIGATION 31: STORING SOLAR ENERGY □ At those times of the year when a solar home depends most on the sun for heat, the days are short and the nights are long. Consequently, ways must be found to store solar energy and release it slowly during those periods when the sun is below the horizon.

To investigate which materials best absorb and hold thermal energy, fill small cans, such as 6-ounce (170 g) frozen-juice cans, halfway with different materials. You might use water, sand, salt, dirt, gravel, sawdust, stones, and lead or copper shot. Place the cans in bright sunlight for several hours. Which material reached the highest temperature? Which material absorbed the most solar energy? Because of mass and specific heat, your answer to these two questions may be quite different.

To see which material best retains heat, place the same cans in a 120° oven until they're all at the same temperature. Be sure to put a metal cover over the water so it can't evaporate.

Remove the cans, place them on a sheet of cardboard on a counter, and record their temperatures at regular intervals as they cool. Which material cools fastest? Slowest? Which materials do you think would be good for storing solar energy?

Project 6: A Bigger Model Solar Home

Design and build a larger, more substantial model solar home. Tinker with it to find ways to reduce the rate that it loses heat and increase the rate that it gains solar energy. What will you use to absorb and store solar energy? Look at and read about real solar homes as you work. Your reading may lead you to make other changes.

What effect would scaling your model up to a full-size home have on the rates of heat loss and gain that you have measured?

CONSERVING ENERGY IS AN ONGOING TASK ■ You've investigated a great many ways to conserve energy. By conserving energy you'll reduce the money you spend for fuel and electricity. You'll also help the nation and world preserve its limited fossil fuels for a longer period and

Stacks of water-filled drums placed at south-facing ends of this solar house in New Mexico absorb sun heat in the daytime and radiate it inward to make the interior of the home comfortably warm.

give scientists, engineers, and inventors time to develop alternative sources of energy that make use of natural energy sources that produce less pollution. This book may have helped you to see the need for conserving energy as well as showing you how to do it. But you've just begun. With experience, you'll continue to find ways to conserve energy. Put your findings to use; the world will thank you!

FOR FURTHER READING

Branley, Franklyn M. *Energy for the Twenty-First Century*. New York: Crowell, 1985.

Butti, Ken, and John Perlin. *A Golden Thread: 2500 Years of Solar Architecture and Technology*. Palo Alto, Calif.: Cheshire Books, 1980.

Gardner, Robert. *Energy Projects for Young Scientists*. New York: Franklin Watts, 1987.

Gipe, Paul. *Wind Energy: How to Use It*. Harrisburg, Pa.: Stackpole, 1983.

Haber-Schaim, Uri. *Energy, a Sequel to IPS*. Englewood Cliffs, N.J.: Prentice-Hall, 1983.

Hassol, Susan, and Beth Richman. *Energy*. Snowmass, Colo.: Windstar Foundation, 1989.

Herda, D. J., and Margaret L. Madden. *Energy Resources: Towards a Renewable Future*. New York: Franklin Watts, 1990.

Keeler, Barbara. *Energy Alternatives*. San Diego, Calif.: Lucent Books, 1990.

Morrison, James W. *The Complete Energy-Saving Home Improvement Guide*. New York: Arco, 1978.

Neal, Philip. *Energy, Power Sources, and Electricity*. North Pomfret, Vt.: David & Charles, 1989.

Oei, Paul D.; Eugene W. Sorenson; and Chih-Ming Chang. *Projects and Experiments in Energy*. New York: National Energy Foundation, 1982.

INDEX

Italicized page numbers refer to
illustrations or tabular matter.